36 1

From Disaster to Distinction:

A REPUBLICAN REBIRTH

By The Ripon Society

A **PB** SPECIAL
PUBLISHED BY POCKET BOOKS
NEW YORK / 1966

Published by Pocket Books, a division of Simon & Schuster, Inc.,
630 Fifth Avenue, New York, N. Y. 10020,
and on the same day in Canada by Pocket Books of Canada, Ltd.,
Richmond Hill, Ontario

Printed in the United States of America

Contents

FOREWORD

Since 1963 the Ripon Society has been a strong and persuasive Republican voice, addressing the intelligence of the party and stimulating its conscience. In this book, the Ripon voice speaks once again to a party which stands at a major crossroads and to a nation which faces momentous decisions.

The young men and women who comprise this research and policy organization have built their analysis on the premise that men *can* learn from history and on the conviction that they *must*. They spent considerable time exploring the history of the Republican party since early 1964, chronicling the painful road to disaster in that year and the subsequent search for recovery and for distinction.

In the first section of the book they diagnose what went wrong in 1964, what the party must *not* do if it wants to play a responsible governing role in the years ahead. In the second section is prescribed a new course for the party, finding some evidence in the 1965 elections of what the party *must* do if it is to help shape the nation's future.

This book is not merely a challenge to Republicans, calling on them to rise above a narrow and outmoded rightist conservatism. It is a challenge to all Americans, daring them to move beyond politics as usual, away from the clichés and categories of all parties of the past four decades and into the tough and exciting realities of the decades to come. It is in that spirit that this book should be read.

An examination of the challenges of tomorrow leads to several important conclusions. I select one in particular for discussion at this point. It is vitally important for us to realize, I believe, that our ability to *personalize* government has not kept pace with our ability to *centralize* it. This should not be interpreted as a call for repeal of centralization. The 1964 election proves that the American political system will not soon endorse the repeal or even the disparagement of the exercise *toward certain ends,* and in varying degree, of centralized power. Our public life today mirrors what businesses, schools, churches, unions have long understood. There

4

are certain values to be gained by focusing and collecting responsibility. A central government can coordinate and rationalize, it can pursue the even-handed incidence of justice, it can mobilize the widest possible assortment of human and economic resources.

While the pull toward centralization is one of the powerful themes of contemporary American life, the past several years have revealed a second and apparently contradictory trend. This is a pull toward decentralization, an impulse which has grown out of an even deeper concern for what I have called the "personalization" or the "humanization" of our large institutions—economic, educational, religious, governmental. There has been an undeniable tendency for such institutions to begin to think once again about the individual human being with whom they deal and the quality of the experiences which they share with him.

If there is tension between these two trends, then we must not be trapped into the easy course of favoring one and fighting the other. We will gain nothing by condemning all centralizing tendencies, for that is reaction. We will gain nothing by rallying localists against nationalists, for that is hopeless.

It is my hope that American leaders in the years ahead will approach this challenge in a new spirit. This tension between centralizing trends and decentralizing impulses can and must be reconciled. What some have seen as gladiatorial combat can become a creative dialogue. Centralization can be personalized and decentralization can be rationalized.

The accomplishment of such a task will require men and parties of unusual intelligence and discipline and sensitivity. While they must appreciate the values and uses of power at all governmental levels, they must be willing to measure the success of their programs in qualitative and not just quantitative terms. They must feel deeply the value of government which involves its citizens and so dignifies their lives. They must understand that state and local governments can be creative and able partners of federal authority and that individual human beings are not "means" in a grand design but the "end" of every program.

It is my conviction that the Republican party stands in a unique position to articulate and implement this philosophy. As the minority party nationally, it is free to take a fresh look at problems and policies. Its rich traditions make it sensitive to many of the values I have mentioned. They are a part of a great Republican legacy.

The importance of reconciling centralization and personalization is evident in many specific situations. The field of civil rights is a notable example. Here federal power has recently been invoked in behalf of racial justice. This was long overdue and most significant. But the fact that several hundred men said "aye" one noon in Washington will not in itself bring dignity and meaning to a Negro or Puerto Rican or Indian neighborhood. Even when these laws are fully implemented, racial justice will still require the establishment of those complex social and economic tissues which alone enable a man or woman to participate meaningfully in the whole life of a society. This is a work which requires imaginative leadership and, ultimately, involvement, the liberating involvement of the people themselves on a local and neighborhood level.

The same considerations affect the problem of poverty. Here again the idea of a federal War on Poverty can inspire a nation, indeed a world. But the idea is not the reality and even now political betrayal dims the lustre of the promise. Programs assertedly for the poor have been treated as opportunities at the trough of political patronage. Urban Democratic machines have taken over the projects and have greedily distorted their purposes. The Democratic mayors of some of our larger cities have openly challenged those in the Administration who would more directly involve the poor in the implementation of their own programs.

The Ripon Society analysis proves quite convincingly that the future of American politics lies in the nation's cities. Republicans should respond to this urban frontier with enthusiasm and alacrity, for here again the Republican legacy is rich in resources. Already the party enjoys a substantial voting base in suburban areas. Republicans have traditionally focused attention and energy at the state, county, and municipal levels while many Democrats have seen such governmental units as irrelevant for reform purposes. One consequence of this attitude is the Democratic failure to govern urban America adequately. In too many of our cities people have been treated as means instead of ends.

I believe that the tragic failure of local government in this country can be reversed. Vital and compassionate leadership can be exercised on the municipal level. Already a new spirit can be seen in New York City, for example, as people come to understand that government is not "those guys" but rather "us guys." One of the most exciting things about the Republican-Liberal mayoralty campaign in 1965 was that it involved people in the political process who had not been involved before. I believe that this new sense of dignity and energy will be a valuable resource for the nation's largest city for many years to come. The Republican party can be an important part of similar renewal in states and localities across the country.

My purpose is to recommend this excellent book to you, the reader. Here are presented the views of the Ripon Society as to where the Republican party should go. Were this a dialogue or book review, rather than a foreword, I would volunteer some comment as to the dilemmas a Republican National Chairman must face as the party confronts these challenges.

Chairman Ray Bliss does not attempt to make policy. Over the years, the National Committee have denied that right to a Chairman. Republican policy today is formulated, in part, by the Congressional leadership, and, in my opinion, articulated best of all by the new Republican Co-ordinating Committee, wherein the Republican Governors also have a voice and an opportunity to be influential.

The National Chairman does not even make the rules. These are formulated at the quadrennial national convention and interpreted by the Executive Committee of the Republican National Committee. The present Executive Committee was appointed by Chairman Bliss's predecessor and its majority speaks for those who were successful at San Francisco in 1964. One hopes, but does not count on, some conversions to a more realistic point of view in this committee. In any event, its personnel will not change until the end of the 1968 convention.

To me, it is evident that Chairman Bliss, driving a team of horses with divergent concepts of what constitutes forward direction, has shown himself to be open minded to—and, fortunately, committed to—new and progressive programs, which include the guidance of the Republican Coordinating Committee, the work sessions on securing more of the big city vote, the appointment of competent deputies, the support of task forces on urban problems, fiscal solutions and other intensive pre-election planning.

But from the vantage point—or disadvantage point—of a former National Chairman, I believe that Mr. Bliss will not do the job for the far right, and he cannot do the ideological job for the rest, the great majority, of his party.

This job can be done, and it must be done, by those in our party who are closest to the voters: precinct workers, party leaders, youth groups, volunteer citizens, and—above all—the candidates for public office, those who are most responsive to the needs of people in their own communities. They are the ones who must do battle for the cause of electing Republicans to office by offering good candidates and by espousing good causes that truly represent the public interest.

Politics in a free society is influenced heavily by the survival of the fittest. Those in the Republican party who best represent the public view will survive—and prevail.

Hugh L Scott

Hugh Scott
*United States Senator
from Pennsylvania
former Chairman of the
Republican National Committee*

EDITOR'S NOTE

THIS BOOK is divided into two sections. The first part recreates the Republican campaign of 1964, analyzing the impact of the Goldwater disaster upon the Republican party. By recalling the style, the strategy, and the results of the Republican Presidential campaign in 1964 we seek to learn the lessons experience may teach us.

The second part of this book discusses the future of the Republican party. It presents a challenge to all Republicans. While we cannot reshape the past, we can mold the future and make it our own. In Part Two, we examine the Republican response to defeat and describe the new ideas and programs the party must advance if it is to serve the nation and revive its fortunes.

The young are given the past, but must earn the right to hold the future. We believe that the Ripon Society has begun the task of shaping the Republican future. We direct this book to the young men and women of the party in the hope that they will join us in this exciting work.

The Ripon Society is a Republican research and policy organization composed of young members of the business, professional, and academic communities. The Society seeks to rally the energies and talents of thinking young people to the cause of constructive Republicanism. It strives to generate creative discussion that will produce a bold and persuasive Republican policy posture. To this end, the Society was active before, during, and after the campaign of 1964, preparing studies, writing speeches, and aiding Republican leaders. This activity continues.

Many Ripon Society members contributed to this book. The manuscript was drafted by Lee W. Huebner (Wisconsin), J. Eugene Marans (Montana), John S. Saloma, III (Massachusetts), and William Wessels (Massachusetts). Valuable editorial assistance was given by Terrence E. Dwyer (Iowa), Robert L. Beal (Massachusetts), Christopher T. Bayley (Washington), Emil H. Frankel (Connecticut), Edward A. C. Dubois (Massachusetts), Alan P. Caplan (Massachusetts), Peter J. Wallison (New York), Theodore S. Curtis (Maine), and others.

9

The Society also wishes to acknowledge the contribution to the preparation of this book made by Republican party officials in many states, our field force of local associates, persons in various centers of higher learning across the country, and Miss Marianne Magocsi, who has given the Society dedicated secretarial assistance.

Thomas E. Petri (Wisconsin), Editor

Persons interested in joining the Ripon Society, assisting it on various research and policy papers in preparation or under consideration, or receiving further information on the Society are invited to write to:

> The Ripon Society
> Box 138
> Cambridge, Massachusetts 02138

Part One

Election '64:
"Into the Political Wilderness"

Republican strength was growing as the party approached 1964. Percentages of the Congressional vote and state legislative seats had increased significantly in 1960 and 1962. The finest group of local and state candidates in over a decade was assembled for the 1964 contest. But high hopes were crushed on November third. The field of candidates was decimated; many potential leaders were lost. Millions of citizens, particularly among the young, made decisions that will affect American politics for a generation and more to come. For once party loyalty has been breached it is exceedingly difficult to recover a meaningful allegiance.

The Republican party lost the presidency by a record margin. Representation in the Senate was reduced to 32 seats out of 100. Republicans in the House numbered 140 out of 435. Almost 500 state legislative seats were sacrificed and countless Republicans were thrown out of elective and appointive positions at the local and state level. Today only one out of four Americans considers himself a Republican compared to 38 percent in 1940 and 30 percent in 1960. In 1964, the Republican party lost an election, forfeited the accumulated gains of years, and risked its very future as a viable force in American politics.

At such a time of crisis it is important that the leaders and members of the Republican party begin the work of reconstruction from a perspective that is both realistic and honest. No one can win the confidence of a demoralized party unless he first admits the extent of the Republican disaster in November, 1964. One cannot be cured until he admits that he is ill. The Republican party must begin its recovery by looking, soberly and candidly, at what has happened to it since 1963.

We undertake this analysis because we are Republicans who want our party to survive and grow. We believe that the millions who worked so hard on behalf of our party—even in such an unrewarding year—are entitled to ask of their leadership, "Why not victory?" We ask that question today as we look at the style, the issues, and the results of Election 1964.

1

S T Y L E:

"An Invitation to Disaster"

THE YEAR 1964 was a strange and bizarre political year. As in Alice's Wonderland many things were as they should not have been and one incredible development followed another.

This was the unhappy year in which the party of Lincoln warmly embraced a racist Democrat from South Carolina and refused even a respectful convention hearing to the Republican Governor of New York.

This was the bizarre year when Goldwater's own son predicted a small stock market collapse if his father won, when the Senator's closest friends confided their troubled fear of "that gang around Goldwater," when the Republican Vice-Presidential candidate observed that "Barry has all the political sophistication of my five-year-old son."

This was the strange year in which even staunch Goldwaterites like George Murphy and Tim Babcock found it best to protect their own candidacies by saying as little as possible about their national ticket.

This was the remarkable year when Vermont went Democratic and Georgia went Republican; a year when Alabamans *could not vote* for an incumbent Democratic President, while millions of Republicans cast their first Democratic presidential vote ever.

This was the frustrating year when a campaign based on morality came to appear immoral, when the cause of a "true" conservative was repudiated in areas that even Governor Wallace had carried, when a campaign possessed by a fear of being an echo left many voters with no real choice at all.

Lyndon Johnson was a vulnerable candidate on several counts—but many voters could find no alternative. Voter participation declined from 1960 levels in thirty-six states, including a drop of 11 percent in North Dakota and 9 percent in Missouri, Massachusetts, and Rhode Island. A bewildered young housewife in Minnesota spoke for millions of Americans when she pleaded, "Can't I vote no?"

The Candidate:

From Out of the West

Whatever his private reservations were, Barry M. Goldwater could never dispel the impression that he was the Messiah of the radical right. No egghead he, but nonetheless the leader of an ideological ferment. He had put his name to books that circulated throughout American suburbs and campuses—forthright and simple books, whose messages were alien to the ears of many who read them. And as these readers dismissed solutions that were out of touch with the economic and social realities of mid-twentieth-century America, they dismissed the author with them. It was a basic mistake. For there were many in the United States of America, as 1964 approached, to whom those blunt words and simple concepts were not alien. They did not always know much about economics or diplomacy, but they did know their own businesses, their own neighborhoods. And more than that, they remembered the simple truths that had seemed to guide the happier society of their childhood. If Goldwater's words were heresy to those who had painfully come to terms with the unpleasantness of a changing world, they were prophecy to those who dared to think that such a reconciliation might yet be avoided, that their illusions might still be spared. To achieve the simpler, better, and freer way of life would require a radical shift in the mood and in the direction of American government, this they knew. It would be difficult to achieve, yet it just might be done—if only the guiding philosophy remained pure enough, if only the leader were steadfast enough, sure enough.

Senator Goldwater was that leader. His language was rough, his candor shocking, his sincerity beyond reproach. He came out of the West like a refreshing breeze. He had a hard jaw and a hard line. He flew his own plane, operated a ham radio, took prize-winning photographs, and spoke Indian languages. He told the housewife that she knew more economics than John Kenneth Galbraith, the businessman that Arthur Schlesinger's access to the White House was a national disgrace. The Eastern seaboard, he said, should be floated away and Harvard should institute the fraternity system in order to protect its young men against Communism. He was the Viceroy independent thinker, the Marlboro man. He donned stetson and blue jeans for the cover of *Life* and boarded a hired palomino.

His chief speech writer, Karl Hess, had written in 1954:

> The question of freedom, when stripped to its steel center, is just this: Who has the guns? It would not be America really if it did not produce men who suddenly tire of palaver and reach for the rifle on the wall.

The Western frontier had produced many such men, and millions of Americans gave thanks when they saw Barry riding into town. He would take the Winchester from over the fireplace and clean out the Kennedy–Johnson gang, the Wall Street bankers, the labor agitators, the Eastern me-tooers who hole up in the Big Government Saloon. And then, would he not face down the bullies in Moscow and Peking and solve all our problems? Of course he would. It was simply a question of courage and self-reliance and superior moral force. Were we not still God's people?

But there were many who did not give thanks. Goldwater was the first choice of less than one out of four Republicans in pre-convention polls. The minority party desperately needed to make their very best campaign effort in 1964. Goldwater could not do it. His voting record, his contradictory statements, his varied writings, whatever their intended meaning, had confused many voters and frightened many more. His history, his temperament, his philosophy had lost millions of votes before the race had ever begun.

The Convention:

Debacle at the Cow Palace

Senator Goldwater won the presidential nomination long before San Francisco. There are those who argue that he had it "sewed up" before the California primary—perhaps before any of the primaries since his able and uncontested organization lined up delegates in state after state.

But, Goldwater lost the presidential election *before* the fall of 1964. Some say he lost it in the spring primaries when he publicly exposed himself on issue after issue. But if not, then it certainly was lost in San Francisco.

Most voters pay little attention to the campaign and the candidates until it all culminates on television at convention time. What happened at the Cow Palace convinced many Americans that those extremists everyone had been hearing about were really in control and were not about to accommodate anyone, not Eisenhower, not Scranton, and certainly not Rockefeller who had fought their hero all the way. They didn't have to go East for *their* money. If the old establishment "wanted in" it would have to come around. The new leaders were not going out of their way to send an invitation.

The first sign came with General Eisenhower's speech. His commendation of Republican senators and congressmen who had worked hard to pass the civil rights bill was greeted with an embarrassing silence that only a few delegations tried vainly to fill with applause. But when he attacked "sensation-seeking columnists and commentators" a bored convention roared to life and the General looked like a lion tamer who had lost his chair and whip. Delegates stood, shook their fists at the press booths, and cursed reporters or cameramen on the floor. The party had its first black eye.

Then came the Goldwater–Laird move to delay the amendments on extremism and nuclear responsibility until the platform had been read in full. This would postpone the speeches of Senator Scott, and Governors Herter, Rockefeller, and Romney until the early morning hours in the eastern half of the country, when people would have gone to bed. To the majority of the delegates and the gallery any compromise on these matters was clearly heresy.

Nelson Rockefeller spoke for the extremist amendment. He was as welcome as Khrushchev at an American Legion Convention. He stepped to the microphone and the convention exploded in boos, catcalls, whistles, and the rhythmic war chant "We want Barry." The New York Governor asked for a plank condemning "extremism" of any sort, "Communist, Ku Klux Klan, or Bircher." The gallery erupted in rage. He spoke of his workers in the California primary who received threatening phone calls and were subjected to "smear and hate literature, strong arm and goon tactics." The booing increased.

Governor Romney's amendment to condemn extremism in general was also shouted down, though Goldwater later admitted that he would have accepted the proposal had he seen it in advance. Later a provision stating that "the authority to use America's nuclear weapons belongs to the President of the United States" was buried under an avalanche of boos.

"This thing has gone too far," Senator Dirksen observed. He had agreed to nominate Senator Goldwater and, somehow, this was the final capitulation. For Dirksen was the ultra-realist in the party. His voice was Never-Never Land, but his feet were on the ground. He knew that his friend and colleague, Lyndon Johnson, would hit all the targets offered by the unfortunate muddle of contradictions that were the public views of Barry Goldwater. But Barry had the delegates and it was too late for Everett McKinley Dirksen to resist the tide. So he nominated "the peddler's grandson." Then came chaos in a rain of golden foil.

The balloting began. The head of the South Carolina delegation spoke: "We are humbly grateful," he said, "that we can do this for America. South Carolina casts sixteen votes for Barry Goldwater." Scranton was defeated better than four to one by a man who was the choice of less than one out of four of the Republican party rank and file.

Soon the candidate himself was on television. Earlier in the day he had called Lyndon Johnson "the biggest faker in the United States." Now he told the country he would not campaign on personal issues. When asked what he thought the important issues would be, he mentioned "crime and violence in the streets." His solution: action "at the federal level with the federal courts enforcing the law." But the Senator was supposed to be the relentless *foe* of "big government" interference in local affairs. Was not public safety one of the more clearly defined local responsibilities? The voters had been introduced to a paradox that they would come to regard as typical.

When the Senator talked of "violence in the streets" did he mean the anticipated Negro riots of the "long, hot summer"? Considering the basis of his electoral strategy, it was hard to think otherwise. The platform committee, loyal to the Senator, had already refused to broaden the civil rights plank in the platform. Jackie Robinson had walked out of the convention. At the height of the Goldwater demonstration, someone tried to set fire to a Negro delegate's coat. Other Negroes complained of being threatened by Goldwater's delegates. The television networks were relating these incidents to the entire country and the party of Lincoln was not looking any brighter.

There remained, of course, the acceptance speech. Surely now the Senator would make some conciliatory gesture to bring the remaining three-fourths of the party under his banner.

General Eisenhower and former Vice-President Nixon were already on the platform, symbolizing the line of succession. "Forget what you've been told; listen to him and make up your own mind," Nixon said in introduction. The stage was set and the nation listened.

> Tonight there is violence in our streets, corruption in our highest offices, aimlessness among our youth, anxiety among our elderly . . . despair among the many who look beyond material success toward the inner meaning of their lives. . . .

All well and good, but then . . .

> Anyone who joins in all sincerity, we welcome. Those who do not care for our cause we do not expect to enter our ranks in

any case. And let our republicanism, so focused and dedicated, not be made fuzzy and futile by unthinking and stupid labels. *I would remind you that extremism in the defense of liberty is no vice! Moderation in the pursuit of justice is no virtue.*

Jaws dropped across the nation. There could be no mistaking the meaning of those words. The Senator preferred purity to power; he was unprepared to make the smallest concession to the moderates. He would rise or fall with the hard core of his followers and that meant he would most assuredly fall. As Goldwater finished his speech, millions of Republicans were sadly resigning themselves to voting Democratic for the first time. On behalf of the Republican party, the Senator from Arizona had just issued an invitation to disaster.

On the floor of the convention they went absolutely wild.

The Campaign:
Passion for Purity

Throughout the campaign, the Republican nominee repeatedly displayed most glaring handicaps. He needed to conciliate moderates; he had virtually read them out of his crusade. He had to reassure millions that he was not an extremist; he had chosen the most important moment of the campaign for a defense of extremism that even his closest supporters now view as a fatal move.

But if the Republican party had a chance for victory when it left San Francisco in July, the opportunity was shattered by one of the most inept and unprofessional campaigns in American political history.* A Research Institute of America poll of thousands of businessmen showed in late October that even among those supporting the Arizona Senator, 52 percent complained that the Republican campaign had been poorly run while an equal number admitted the effectiveness of the Democratic effort. As journalist Robert J. Donovan puts it: "Senator Goldwater ran a campaign that was so bad that it was difficult to regard him as a serious candidate for the President of the United States." One Goldwater aide confessed late in the fall that even he was tempted to vote against the GOP candidate: "If a man can't run a campaign," he sighed, "how can he run the country?"

What went wrong? At the heart of Republican campaign problems was the fact that the Goldwater leadership exercised an

---

* Goldwater lieutenant Stephen Shadegg has documented the chaos within the organization in his book, *What Happened to Goldwater?* Holt, Rinehart, and Winston, 1965

oppressive exclusiveness that put loyalty to a small cabal ahead of loyalty to the Republican party.

Like most ideological movements, the Goldwater crusade worried more about commitment and purity than it did about ability or efficiency. In the late 1950s Goldwater had promised never to run for the presidency because "I am not a college graduate" and he thought this should be a minimum qualification for the office "in this day and age." Rightly or wrongly his followers changed his mind. The operating premise became: "Their strength will be as the strength of ten if only their hearts are pure." But as the Arizona Mafia turned away competent moderates and welcomed inexperienced extremists they found that it didn't always work that way.

The Goldwater high command purged the national committee staff of many skilled and loyal workers whose talents would be sorely missed in the ensuing weeks. It cut itself off from the entreaties and advice of countless party regulars. Experienced Goldwater professionals like Wayne Hood and F. Clifton White were ignored on important policy matters. The national chairmanship was given to a young politician who had never served as a county chairman, a total stranger to most Republican professionals. He completed the purge by appointing a new executive committee, removing experienced leaders from states like Michigan, Minnesota, and Wisconsin and appointing new members from Mississippi, Louisiana, and Arizona.

Such exclusiveness worked to isolate and weaken the Goldwater leadership clique. In their passion for purity they neglected the fundamental requirement of political leadership—the need to respect the complexity and diversity of a great party. They made no attempt to win the confidence of those whom they had defeated in San Francisco. Rather than reaching out to the moderates, Goldwater's selection of the vice-presidential candidate only emphasized their repudiation. Less than eight months after the assassination of President Kennedy had demonstrated the importance of the vice-presidency, Goldwater chose as his running mate a man with no important qualification for the office. His reason: "Bill Miller drives Lyndon nuts." Miller's response: "Barry's a Protestant and a Jew and I'm a Catholic and anyone who votes against that ticket is a damned bigot."

On election day William Miller lost even his own Congressional district by 73,000 votes while the Republican candidate to succeed him in the House was winning by 9,000.

The blight that these irregular tactics produced was not confined to the national ticket. Throughout the campaign, little political attention or financial support was given to state and local Republican candidates. The Senate and House Campaign Committees were told to sink or swim on their own as most funds were cut off. Loyal party workers were ignored or purged in many states; private Goldwater committees often bypassed state organizations. Connecticut, New York, Indiana, and North Dakota were but a few of the states where prominent Goldwater supporters flirted openly with opponents of Republican candidates.

In Connecticut, Republican Senate candidate John Davis Lodge found himself in the unusual position of running against a man who was endorsed by both the Americans for Democratic Action and the Young Americans for Freedom. Moreover, a national chairman of the Citizens for Goldwater Committee supported his Democratic opponent. Senator Goldwater never did endorse Republican senatorial candidate Richard May in Virginia.

But the supreme irony, after sacrificing so much to keep the faith without compromise or contamination, was that the message did not come through! Issues were crucial to the voters, but not in the way the conservatives had thought. The simple bracing answers now seemed to answer nothing. A host of qualifications and excuses blurred the once-hard line. The charm and candor of the candidate were muffled. An unreal tone came over the entire campaign.

Goldwater and Miller scattered their fire widely. They shifted emphasis erratically from day to day, achieving little continuity and no momentum. Positions on issues were presented at the very times and places where they would do the ticket the most harm. Even his closest supporters noted increasingly during the campaign that the Senator read his speeches stoically. Nor could his ineffective speechwriters provide him with the eloquence his campaign so desperately needed.

Goldwater's rhetoric confused the debate and left him vulnerable to charges of name calling, smearing, and carelessness. He tried and failed to get additional mileage from the tired charge that the Democrats were "soft on communism." He told the nation that Democrats in Milwaukee were "fascists" because they did not allow "a diversity of views" in their organization. He thought he could persuade the American people to elect him to the most powerful and distinguished office on earth by telling them that President Kennedy had contrived the whole Cuban missile crisis of 1962 in order to win the congressional elections.

Goldwater and Miller were on the defensive through the entire campaign, apologizing for earlier statements or defending against Democratic charges. Much of the final week was spent rationalizing the projected defeat. Post-election reports tell us that the Goldwater high command had conceded defeat several days before the election and had cut planned activities to save money. The already slow pace grew even slower, hurting many Republicans in close state and local races. Later, Republican candidates and workers found boasts of a treasury surplus ironic when they remembered how little money was available in the fall.

Throughout the autumn, Goldwater was never allowed to speak informally—nor even to motorcade in most instances. The charm and good humor that Goldwater had used effectively in building his national image were useless to him in such a campaign. The Goldwater leadership went out of its way to poison relationships with the news media. Rudeness in San Francisco, the isolation-ward policy whereby reporters were banned from party headquarters in Washington, the refusal of the Senator to schedule a single regular press conference during his campaign—these were manifestations of a hostile and suspicious attitude that, whatever its supposed justification, was very bad politics indeed.

The campaign was bizarre in other regards. At its peak Senator Goldwater had to absolve his staff of responsibility for an expensive "morality" film that he himself labeled a "racist appeal." One of his public-relations directors, Russell Walton, described it as an appeal to "raw, naked emotions." The film was designed to remind the American public of "the rising crime rate, rising juvenile delinquency, narcotics, pornography, filth magazines . . . wife trading, the jet set, and the whole damned ratpack situation. . . . We just want to make them mad, make their stomachs turn," he said. It is distressing to realize that the Goldwater lieutenants found such appeals appropriate in a campaign for the Presidency of the United States.

In the latter stages of the campaign, the commendable Republican poll-watching efforts were misused in several localities. A crude attempt to have Negro voters waste their ballots by writing in the name of Martin Luther King was quickly linked in press reports to an employee of the Republican National Committee.

A shameful wave of trash literature appeared in Republican headquarters around the country—written, as the Executive Director of the Fair Campaign Practices Committee put it, "through a 'steaming mirage of hate.'" Experienced Republican professionals cringed when Goldwater precinct captains made their reports: "It's 200 for Johnson and 100 for Goldwater, but we've got lots of 'don't knows' that we're going to take the books around to next week." The chances were very good, the pros realized, that "the books" would drive most of the "don't knows" right over into the Democratic column. And they did.

It is ironic and sad that the man who led the Republican party to defeat in 1964 is the same man who rose to power on the strength of his passion and promise for victory. Senator Goldwater had taken much pride in the Republican renaissance that he now so abruptly terminated. We grieve with him as we survey the remnants of our party. But the fact that the man who led us in 1964 once shared our triumphs and buoyed our hopes does not excuse his responsibility for the desolation and the ruin.

The unreality of the 1964 campaign can be attributed, we believe, to the private and unreal vision of the Goldwater leaders. Theirs was a dream of a political world without politics. It was a dream that lured them away from the canons of party regularity. It beguiled them into foolish statements and foolish decisions. It was a dream that was impatient with the desires of the American voter. It led the Goldwater command to believe stubbornly and against all scientific evidence that there was a hidden conservative vote that would save them all at the final hour. Thus, they spoke knowingly of "private polls," continually and recklessly misestimated their chances, and even worried toward the end whether the Senator had "peaked" his campaign too soon. A private and unreal vision sustained them from the very beginning, but at the final hour it let them down.

There is important evidence to indicate that the Goldwater leadership has not yet left that world of dreams, for what else can now convince them that the unprecedented disaster of 1964 was really a moral victory?

We believe that the Republican party should not again entrust its future to such leadership. The goals of a minority that seeks ideological conversion through uncompromising zeal must be respected. But under no conditions can such goals become those of a major party that must seek political effectiveness through accommodation and reasoned cooperation.

So it was that the campaign of 1964 was everything it should not have been. At a time when the American people needed an incisive critique of Democratic programs, a full airing of issues, a constructive and creative dialogue on critical problems, at such a time they were treated instead to one of the dullest, emptiest, lowest level campaigns in the history of American presidential politics. The whole cast of the Republican effort was too often amateurish, almost never profound, occasionally tasteless, and almost always ineffective. The great lesson we have learned from the election of 1964 is that we don't want to go through another like it.

2

STRATEGIES AND ISSUES:

"The Goldwater Plan in Action"

GOLDWATER strategists passionately believed that the Democratic coalition, formed by Franklin Roosevelt in the thirties, was breaking up. A real "conservative" could deliver millions of silent voters from years of frustration and shatter the coalition forever. Senator Goldwater was the only man who could do it.

The new consensus of resurgent "conservatives" would be regional. M. Stanton Evans of the Indianapolis *News* handed down the gospel. There would be no appeal "to a mythical average person of the Gallup poll findings," but rather "to majorities in a constellation of states adding up to a majority in the Electoral College." The South, the border states, the Midwest, plains states, and the Rockies would be the stars of this new heaven. Moreover, postwar gains in the cities and suburbs would be increased, farmers would rediscover their true political home, small businessmen, professional men, and the new money of the West would rally under the Goldwater banner.

The Senator had much to offer. He appealed to those who yearned for a genuine confrontation of the Right and the Left, and to those who desired to reward a faithful party conservative. Best of all, he could seize control of the party from the Eastern establishment and the unbroken dynasty of me-tooers that had ruled it since 1940. Running as a "real" Republican, Goldwater would revive the "silent vote" and sweep into the presidency with state and local candidates happily riding his coattails.

The future of the "conservative cause" was the primary concern. One of the biggest factors in Goldwater's decision to seek the presidency was his conviction that he could win at least 45 percent of the popular vote and leave the movement a permanent base on which to build for future elections. (He actually won only 38.5 percent.)

In *The Winning Side: The Case for Goldwater Republicanism*, Goldwater biographer Ralph de Toledano argued that a break with eastern Republicans was essential if the party expected to develop "strong and necessary ties with the new and enlightened conservative South." The Draft Goldwater Committee accordingly declared its independence from eastern Republicans and concentrated its efforts on the South and West.

Believing that the desired majority could not be engineered without dedicated conservatives in control of party machinery, the Goldwater forces pursued a policy of intra-party conflict. To accentuate the impression of a clear choice, the moderates had to be purged from party leadership.

By mid-1963, the conservatives controlled the leadership and staff of the National Committee and were laying the groundwork for a Goldwater candidacy. Following the dictates of the regional strategy, they changed the Eisenhower-era Operation Dixie into a militantly conservative all white southern Republican organization; and they de-emphasized appeals to the big city, Negro, and labor votes.

The Goldwater strategy was designed to emphasize six major issues: hostile reaction to the civil rights movement; the weakness of the administration's foreign policy; the ballooning of the federal bureaucracy and national debt; the ineptitude of Secretary Freeman's agricultural policy; Secretary McNamara's dictatorship of the defense establishment; and "religion, morality, and justice." It would be a consensus of discontent.

The morality issue was thought to have particular appeal. Goldwater would denounce the Supreme Court's prayer decision, the corrupt political machines, and the soaring crime rate. The "breakdown of law and order" and the coddling of "obviously guilty" criminals were interpreted as products of thirty years of liberal misrule. Tie it all together: Billy Sol Estes, Bobby Baker, a Democratic president who drives recklessly. Give them Goldwater and the party will ride into the White House on a wave of moral indignation.

Ralph de Toledano told us why the Senator would win:

> He represents a new mood in American politics. He is the symbol of conservatism on the march—the conservatism of young intellectuals who have . . . seen the Democratic future and know it doesn't work . . . The great middle class which made this country and sustains it today cries for Barry Goldwater because he thinks in concrete terms of their problems.

This, then, was the basic strategy—weld the new conservatism of the South and the West into a solid majority, capture the great middle class of the suburbs and the cities, win back the farmer, give the dissatisfied young intellectual the cause he has hungered for and the Goldwater "charisma" would do the rest. The dedication of the conservatives would turn the campaign into a crusade and Republicans would sweep to victory.

It was nice to think so anyway.

The 1964 Campaign:
The Goldwater Strategy

The campaign followed the "conservative" strategy and, except in parts of the South, all of its assumptions were proved wrong.

There was no hidden conservative vote. As the Republican National Committee concluded in its detailed summary of the 1964 elections, "the belief that there exists a huge, silent vote which had not voted previously but which, under the right conditions, would emerge as a new balance of power in Presidential elections," was proved false.*

The anticipated regional coalition never developed. Senator Goldwater won only the states that went to the Dixiecrats in 1948 plus Georgia and his home state of Arizona.** President Johnson pre-empted the center and siphoned off the normally Republican suburban vote. He attracted business and professional people, white- and blue-collar voters, and created a truly national coalition.

Republican candidates at all levels found the Goldwater candidacy more harmful than helpful. Many ran as independents; others wish they had. Robert L. Gavin, who lost his bid for the governorship of North Carolina, summarized the problems of many Republicans running under the shadow of Goldwater when he spoke at a meeting of the Republican Governors' Association in December, 1964.

> We had a good program developed to offer the people of North Carolina. . . . But just as these ideas began to catch on and were receiving support . . . I found myself having to constantly defend the national ticket's positions . . . in domestic issues like agricultural support and social security . . . foreign policy questions relating to control of nuclear weapons. . . . But what was most critical was the civil rights question.

The conservatives' prediction that their strategy would command the unified support of Republicans across the country remains a puzzle to this day. The Goldwater–Miller–Burch leadership failed

---

* The 1964 Elections, October, 1965, p. 1.

** In a statement distributed to Republican leaders in June, 1964, the Ripon Society forecast that Senator Goldwater could not count on carrying any state outside the South except Arizona.

to conciliate the moderates and left the party divided and demoralized.

But the basic flaw of the conservative position was the weakness of their candidate. At best, Senator Goldwater was an attractive local politician playing out of his local league. He suggested the sale of TVA while in Knoxville, attacked the administration's poverty bill in Appalachia, and condemned medicare in St. Petersburg. Careless statements about Social Security, nuclear weapons, and farm price supports created fear of radical change and impulsive action. Goldwater's stand on these important issues alienated many people who were expected to vote for him. For the first time in forty years, Democrats became the apparent defenders of the status quo.

The writing off of the Negro vote was the most glaring weakness of the conservative strategy. The Negro vote proved critical in hundreds of contests, North and South. Moreover, many northern white Republicans voted for President Johnson as a matter of "conscience."

On the other hand, Goldwater did propose a five-year program of tax cuts, a plan for returning federal income to the states, and constructive suggestions for changing the draft. But he had little or nothing constructive to say about education, civil rights, conservation, housing, poverty, health, and employment.

Because the long-awaited confrontation of issues did not take place, many observers decided that personalities dominated the campaign. Nevertheless, the people were thinking about issues. A distinguished scholar in the field of voting analysis, Professor Ithiel de Sola Pool of the Massachusetts Institute of Technology, reports that the election *was* dominated by issues rather than by personality or social stratification. His simulmatics computer analysis leads him to the conclusion that "whatever the contents of the campaign output, the voters to an extraordinary extent cast their votes on issues." In 1960, religion, ethnic origin, and past vote were the major factors in voting patterns. In 1964, these were replaced by civil rights, nuclear responsibility, and social welfare legislation. The study concludes: "Barry Goldwater . . . offered the voters a choice of something it was clear they did not want. The result was a landslide in which millions of voters broke from their traditional party, many for the first time in their lives."* Recent elections indicate that voters get excited about the issues only when they have a strong reaction against one candidate's

---

* Ithiel de Sola Pool, Robert Abelson, and Samuel Popkin, *Candidates, Issues and Strategies: A Computer Simulation of the 1960 and 1964 Presidential Election,* Cambridge, Mass., M.I.T. Press, 1965.

position or when the issues are sharply polarized. In 1964, most voters reacted strongly against Goldwater's views.

To offset this public hostility, the Senator stressed a new morality, safety in the streets, prayers in the schools, and personal integrity in public office. Instead of defining clear policies on important national issues, the Goldwater high command tried to base the campaign on his "private principles." The fact of the matter was that Negroes were more interested in what he could do for civil rights in his public role as president than they were in his private convictions against bigotry and his efforts to hire Negroes at his Phoenix department store.

Professor Aaron Wildavsky of the University of California at Berkeley considers the Goldwater campaign a "privatisation" of politics. In this analysis of the Goldwater phenomenon, Wildavsky discusses the Senator's "purist" approach:

> The private conscience of the leader rather than his public responsibilities becomes the focal point of politics. . . . Problems are dealt with by stating one's first principles and assuming that they must be relevant to whatever is in hand. . . . The pragmatic spirit is completely lacking. . . . If only one has principles and stands up for them . . . the messy world of politics—compromise, bargaining, exception, modifications, inconsistencies—will disappear. Political style thus becomes a substitute for politics itself.*

The Republican strategy in 1964 allowed Lyndon Baines Johnson to win the biggest electoral majority in presidential history.

Civil Rights, the Negro, and the Churches:
A Case Study of the Goldwater
Strategy and Its Impact

The four years since the Kennedy–Nixon contest of 1960 had seen a revolution in race relations, culminating in the Civil Rights Act of 1964. When Senator Goldwater's personal interpretation of the Constitution led him to vote against the bill, civil rights became the most potent domestic issue at the Republican Convention as well as in the presidential campaign.

According to highly reliable polls made during the campaign, Senator Goldwater's position on civil rights alienated more voters

---

* Aaron Wildavsky, The Goldwater Phenomonon: Purists, Politicians, and the Future of the American Two Party System, Berkeley, California, manuscript.

than did his position on any other domestic issue. Goldwater charged on the Senate floor that the public accommodations and equal employment sections of the Civil Rights Act "fly in the face of the Constitution and . . . require for their effective execution the creation of a police state." The Supreme Court has since disagreed. At the same time, the responsible leadership of the nation, and of the South, was publicly urging voluntary compliance with the provisions of the bill. The Senator's vote against the civil rights legislation clearly distinguished his position from that of the President and a majority of Republicans in Congress. His vote was a major factor in Governor William Scranton's decision to challenge the Senator for the Republican nomination.

During the campaign, Senator Goldwater pledged to execute the Civil Rights Act if elected. Nevertheless, as the contest drew to a close, he repeatedly attacked the law for threatening "unfair discrimination in the private affairs of men." Proclaimed Senator Goldwater to a Cleveland audience: "I am unalterably opposed to such discrimination, but I also know that government can provide no lasting solution. . . . Government can do little more than offer moral leadership and persuasion. The ultimate solution lies in the hearts of men." He repeated these sentiments in a television appeal broadcast regionally to the southern states in the last few days of the campaign.

The Senator's objections to "legislating morality," his attacks on the Supreme Court, his defense of states' rights, and his discussion of "crime in the streets," all were widely interpreted as anti-civil rights appeals. Eventually, his campaign strategists became so mesmerized by this issue that they produced the now infamous "morality" film which the Senator himself had to repudiate as a "racist appeal."

The restraint of the Negro community in the face of the Goldwater campaign is one of the remarkable stories of the 1964 campaign. Few civil rights supporters demonstrated against Goldwater; they almost completely boycotted his campaign functions. But, on November 3, the Negroes of America waited in long, silent lines to register one of the greatest protest votes ever recorded.

Evidence of Goldwater's alienation of Negro and church groups was clear long before the election. On October 13, four days before Goldwater's major anti-civil rights speech of the campaign, 725 Episcopal bishops, priests, and laymen released an unofficial statement accusing Senator Goldwater and former National Chairman Miller of a "transparent exploitation of racism." In the widely distributed document, the Episcopalians charged that the Republican ticket was "ambitious to be elected by inheriting the votes of the white racists, cultivating and harvesting the white backlash" and that Goldwater and Miller "have sought to frighten citizens by equating the Negro struggle for freedom with crime and violence in the streets while . . . encouraging disrespect for law and order by their own expressed contempt for the federal judiciary, especially for the United States Supreme Court."

In late September, an eighteen-man panel of distinguished Protestant theologians led by Dr. Reinhold Niebuhr, in an editorial in *Christianity and Crisis,* endorsed the President over Senator Goldwater, breaking a twenty-five-year precedent of the magazine. "We point simply to the objective unarguable conflict between his [Senator Goldwater's] record and the judgments of the Christian churches on most of the major issues of social ethics in our time." The group cited the Senator's vote against the Civil Rights Act of 1964 as an example of the "incontrovertible" clash between his views and those of most churches.

And on October 11, fifty of the country's most prominent lawyers joined in a statement deploring Senator Goldwater's campaign attacks on the Supreme Court. The group of lawyers, evenly divided between Republicans and Democrats and including ten law school deans and five former presidents of the American Bar Association, noted that Goldwater's "broadside attacks on the integrity and competence of the Supreme Court . . . overpass the limits of comment appropriate to a presidential candidate [and] . . . are not based on reasoned analysis of the Court's opinions."

Throughout the campaign the Negro leadership of the country vigorously attacked Goldwater's civil rights stand. The Reverend Dr. Martin Luther King took to the campaign trail for the first time in his career to work for a "crushing" defeat of the Republican ticket. Roy Wilkins, longtime executive secretary of the National Association for the Advancement of Colored People, revealed that his organization had dozens of workers distributing millions of pieces of anti-Goldwater get-out-the-vote literature. However, the NAACP did support a number of Republican congressional candidates who had fought for the civil rights bill, such as Representatives John V. Lindsay (New York), William M. McCulloch (Ohio), Charles McC. Mathias, Jr. (Maryland), and Senator Hugh Scott (Pennsylvania).

The Southern Strategy:

"Operation Dixie" Becomes Lily-White

Operation Dixie, which had its roots in the Eisenhower-Nixon administration, had been a serious effort to build Republican party strength in the urban and suburban areas of the new South. It was an appeal to a dynamic element of the southern population based on the economic policies of the Republican administration, and was unapologetic for the Republican record of steady progress in civil rights.

But Operation Dixie was drastically changed with the gradual takeover of the officers and staff of the Republican National Committee by Goldwater supporters after the 1960 election.*

The National Committee channeled large amounts of money into its Southern Division in accord with the Goldwater presidential strategy. As a result, the projects concerning minorities, labor, and big cities were starved for funds. Former National Chairman William Miller told a 1963 meeting of General Eisenhower's Republican Citizens Committee that at least $600,000 had been spent on Operation Dixie since 1958, most of that within the two previous years. Less than one-third that amount was spent on the Minorities Division over the same time.

The new goals for Operation Dixie were summarized by Senator Goldwater's infamous statement before an Atlanta press conference in November, 1961: "We're not going to get the Negro vote as a bloc in 1964 or 1966, so we ought to go hunting where the ducks are." The "ducks" were to be the 128 electoral votes of the Old Confederacy and the hunting expedition inevitably became lily-white. Operation Dixie had few Negroes in its leadership despite the fact 13 percent of the registered voters in the South were Negro, and their number was increasing at a fast rate.

The Negro became excluded from the plans of the National Committee. By 1963, *The Republican Southern Challenge,* Operation Dixie's monthly newsletter, contained virtually no mention of the southern Republican Negro leadership. Efforts by the Minorities Division of the Republican National Committee to establish a Republican Negro newsletter were tabled by Chairman Miller.

In spite of important gains in the Negro Republican vote in the 1963 municipal election in such cities as Louisville, Baltimore, St. Louis, and Kansas City, no significant efforts were made to coordinate the activities of Operation Dixie and the Minorities Division. No Negro Republican leader was invited to the June, 1963, meeting of the Republican National Committee in Denver, held at the height of the Birmingham crisis. Although the nation was then experiencing the most significant racial crisis since the Civil War, the resolution adopted at the Denver meeting had no word of support for the Negro movement. It was difficult to miss the contrast between this Republican inaction and the activity of the

---

* See "Goldwater Supporters Hold Key Professional GOP Posts" *Congressional Quarterly Weekly Report,* No. 41, week ending Oct. 11, 1963, pp. 1770-1774.

Democratic National Committee. The latter appointed Negro journalist Louis Martin as Deputy Chairman and gave him broad
authority to attract Negro votes in all parts of the country through
the use of newsletters, press releases, bulletins, and personal
contacts.

The final act of exclusion came at the San Francisco Convention.
The civil rights amendments to the platform, supported by the
forty-one Negro delegates, were overwhelmingly voted down. Platform Chairman Congressman Melvin Laird was reportedly so in-
censed with George A. Parker (District of Columbia), the Negro
delegate on the platform committee, when he pressed Senator Goldwater for his views on civil rights that he refused to include a plank
on the District of Columbia in the party platform. Some Negroes
were physically attacked on the convention floor.

Before the election, many of these Negro delegates organized the
National Negro Republican Assembly, composed of about 250
Negro leaders from across the country. They supported Republican
candidates whose views were "compatible with the thinking and
legitimate aspirations of Negro citizens" and they voiced their un-
equivocal opposition to Senator Goldwater. The Assembly's prin-
cipal objective was to "create a new atmosphere within the frame-
work of the Republican Party that will make it unmistakably clear
that the Negro citizen is needed, wanted and welcome."

But the Goldwater–Miller–Burch campaign proceeded without
any significant Negro participation. As Negro Americans watched in
amazement, the Minorities Division of the National Committee was
dissolved; and the single Goldwater effort to attract Negro votes
created bizarre repercussions.

An eight-page pamphlet entitled *What About Civil Rights and
Barry Goldwater?* praising Goldwater's personal civil rights record
and assailing that of Johnson, was circulated in September by the
Goldwater–Miller District of Columbia campaign headquarters. The
pamphlet was reportedly printed and distributed at Goldwater's
suggestion to attract the votes of Washington's Negro voters who
outnumber white voters 90,000 to 85,000. Nearly half of the 50,000
copies had been distributed when the Goldwater strategists suddenly ordered the pamphlet withdrawn. According to Carl Shipley,
the District of Columbia GOP Chairman, "the National Committee
was worried about the reverse-circulation problem"—Democrats
were distributing the pamphlet in the South to persuade white
southerners to vote for Johnson. Goldwater strategists also feared
the Democrats would publicly refute the accuracy of the pamphlet
and recommended that Shipley postpone the distribution of the
remaining copies until four days before the election. So heavily
were the Goldwater strategists counting on the white backlash vote,

that they could not risk widespread publicity of the Senator's limited civil rights accomplishments.

Nothing could be more shortsighted, however, than the crude attempt during the campaign to persuade millions of Negro voters to indicate their votes by writing in the name of Reverend Dr. Martin Luther King, Jr., for president. An aide of the Republican National Committee was indicted under New Jersey law for ordering 1.5 million copies of a leaflet urging Negroes to write in King's name. He was acquitted in June, 1966, although others involved in the case were never identified. A series of radio announcements was arranged for broadcast in eleven cities by a front called the Committee for Negroes in Government. It was, as Dr. King said, "a cruel and vicious attempt to confuse Negro voters and nullify their votes." No apology was offered by the Republican National Committee or its leadership to Nobel laureate King.

The southern strategy was a weird and frightening experience for the party of Lincoln. Even as late as January, 1964, on *Meet the Press,* Senator Goldwater could claim that "the South has been turning towards the Republican party, not because the Republican party is a racist party, because you couldn't outrace the Democratic party in the South." In the 1964 election, however, the Goldwater–Miller–Burch strategy finally proved that the elephant could "outrace" the donkey and the rooster across the southland.

Civil Rights and the Negro Vote:
The Anatomy of Electoral Disaster

The 1964 election served as the testing ground of the Republican National Committee's southern strategy. Its implicit anti-civil rights appeal attracted significant support only in rural redneck areas and scattered low-income industrial sections of the South. Elsewhere the effects were disastrous.

A whole new generation of Negro voters was alienated from the Republican party at a time when Negro registration was at an all-time high of 6 million persons. Of these, nearly 2.2 million live in the South, double the number of southern Negroes qualified to vote in 1960. According to the Southern Regional Council, 73.4 percent of registered Negroes voted in 1964. Moreover, the 1965 Voting Rights Act will further expand the Negro vote. By 1968, Negro registration in the South is expected to total more than 3 million—about 20 percent of the southern electorate.

Registration drives throughout the country netted 750,000 new Negro voters by 1964, nearly all of them enrolled in the Democratic party. One example was Baltimore, which registered 27,575 Negroes, 94 percent of whom declared themselves to be Democrats.

The Republican party had maintained considerable Negro support for thirty years after Franklin D. Roosevelt's 1932 victory. President Eisenhower carried 39 percent of the nonwhite vote in 1956, and Richard Nixon retained 32 percent in 1960. Though few GOP leaders noticed it, northern, middle-class Negroes shifted toward the Republican party during the fifties. About 20 percent called themselves Republicans in the early part of the Eisenhower administration; 31 percent did by 1958. Support for Republicans was most striking among Negro independents in the northeast. In 1956, Eisenhower won 70 percent of their vote.*

Yet in 1964, under Goldwater–Miller, the Republican share of the Negro vote dropped to 6 percent, the largest GOP percentage loss among any single group. Southern Negro precincts which had given Eisenhower impressive majorities, and which had gone to Nixon in 1960, rejected Goldwater–Miller by astounding margins. In Richmond, for example, Negroes who had given Nixon 37 percent of their vote in 1960 presented Goldwater with 0.7 percent.**

The undertow effect was also evident in northern Negro precincts. In Illinois the Republican percentage of Negro votes for president fell from 24 percent in 1960 to 3 percent in 1964. In Ohio it went from 29 percent to 3.4 percent, in Michigan from 15 percent to 2 percent, in New York from 26 percent to 4 percent.

The defeat of Robert Taft, Jr., by Senator Stephen M. Young of Ohio was clearly the result of an overwhelming Negro vote against Goldwater, despite Taft's vigorous support of the 1964 civil rights bill. Young's plurality was about 17,000. The estimated Negro vote for the Senator was 250,000. *If Taft had obtained only 4 percent more of this Negro vote, he would have won.*

In Cincinnati, Congressman Carl W. Rich was defeated for re-election in the First Congressional District because his Democratic opponent, John J. Gilligan, took almost all of the 25,000 Negro votes. Rich also voted for the civil rights bill. It was the first time since 1936 that the District elected a Democrat. *If Rich had obtained only 10 percent of the Negro vote, he would have won.*

But the South itself provides the most telling critique of the Goldwater southern strategy.

Senator Goldwater lost Florida, Texas, Tennessee, and Virginia, all of which had supported Eisenhower or Nixon in recent years.

* "Negro Voters in Northern Cities," Simulmatics Report No. 1, May, 1960.
** "The 1964 Elections: A Summary Report with Supporting Tables," Republican National Committee, October, 1965, p. 47.

Goldwater won fewer electoral votes in the South than either Eisenhower or Nixon—he lost six of the eleven southern states.

The Negro vote that Goldwater forfeited was crucial to these results. Only in Johnson's home state of Texas did the Democratic party receive a clear majority of southern white votes. Barry Goldwater did not carry any state where more than 45 percent of the eligible Negroes were registered. Moreover, the Goldwater–Miller ticket lost all of the border states. Republicans did not gain *a single* new senate or congressional seat in any border state in 1964.

While Republicans gained five members of Congress in Alabama and one in Georgia and one in Mississippi, they lost two in Texas, resulting in a net gain of five in the South. All twelve southern and border state Democrats who voted *for* the civil rights bill were re-elected. Of the fourteen southern Republicans who opposed the civil rights bill, three were defeated—Snyder (Kentucky), and Alger and Foreman (Texas). Thirteen southern Republican congressional candidates were defeated in large part by Negro votes.

Republicans lost the southern city and suburban vote in which President Eisenhower had made substantial gains in 1952 and 1956. In Atlanta, Charlotte, Richmond, Orlando, Houston, and the other metropolitan centers of the South, Goldwater ran well behind the best Eisenhower and Nixon performances. The Goldwater–Miller–Burch strategy succeeded in trading off the progressive, industrialized urban areas of the new South for the segregationist, rural regions of the deep South. For Florida, North Carolina, Kentucky, and Texas the GOP received Alabama, Georgia, Mississippi, and Louisiana. Republicans appealed in 1964 to those disappearing areas which represent the southern past; by doing so they were weakened in those key areas which represent the southern future.

The Republican Future in the South

Republican strength in the South did not increase in 1964. The new areas of "Republican" strength cannot provide a durable base for southern republicanism. The Dixiecrat states are traditionally unstable in presidential elections. Their future support of the Republican party will probably be contingent upon the type of appeals that were made in 1964. Furthermore, according to an AP report, Republican gains in the South in November 1964 were restricted to about 100 counties in which Negroes constitute a majority of the population but few are registered to vote. Although the Negroes in these counties have systematically been denied the vote for a century, under the new civil rights law substantially larger percentages will be registered by 1966 and 1968.

In Georgia, Louisiana, and South Carolina Goldwater Republican majorities of 54 percent, 57 percent, and 59 percent of the vote respectively could easily be wiped out in the next election by as little as 40 percent additional Negro registration. In Mississippi and Alabama, where the Republican vote was landslide proportions (87 percent and 69 percent), Negro registration stands at 6 percent and 23 percent respectively.

Any doubts that southern Republicans had about the potency of the Negro vote were dispelled on November 3, 1964. Robert L. Gavin, losing Republican gubernatorial candidate in North Carolina, in a speech to the Republican Governors' Association in Denver a month after the election, noted:

> What was most critical in my campaign was the civil rights question. As best that I can determine, I received about three percent of the 200,000 Negro votes cast in North Carolina and yet my record and positions were more progressive in this area than my opponent's! . . . *This I believe was because of the determination of the Negro race to defeat our national ticket.* No one man can spot his opponent 200,000 votes in North Carolina right from the start and expect to win. In my race it was decisive. . . . The Negro vote is increasing rapidly. From 200,000 in North Carolina at this time it will be 250,000 in 1966 and possibly 300,000 in 1968. I do not believe that we can ignore this vote which is going to increase more and more in the future. I believe as an American, as a Southerner, and as a Republican that this party must be broad enough and positive enough in its principles and platforms to appeal to all voters of the nation. [Italics added]

There were also significant indications of increased southern moderation on civil rights. In Tennessee, where two Senate seats were up at the same time, civil rights bill supporter Ross Bass ran as well as civil rights bill opponent Albert Gore. Similarly, in Texas, Democrat Ralph W. Yarborough, who supported the 1964 bill, won another Senate term by 329,621 votes.

Only in Arkansas was there a truly bright side to the 1964 Republican effort in the South. Republican gubernatorial candidate Winthrop Rockefeller discovered little resistance among whites to implementation of the Civil Rights Act in Arkansas, and directed his appeal to both whites and Negroes. Despite the Johnson sweep, Negroes gave about 60 percent of their votes to Rockefeller in his race against Orval Faubus. As the southern strategy crumbled, the Negroes of Pine Bluff, Arkansas, gave 97.8 percent of their vote to President Johnson and 88.5 percent to Winthrop Rockefeller.

In assessing the impact of this shift, it is vital to remember that while Republicans do not need a majority of the Negro vote to win in either the North or South, they do need a healthy percentage of it. As Senator Thruston B. Morton (R. Ky.) told the Republican National Committee in December, 1962: "When a Republican gets 40 percent of the [Negro] vote, he can win anywhere." A Republican national ticket getting less than 20 percent of the Negro vote, he added, is in serious trouble. The Goldwater–Miller percentage (6 percent) was fatal to Republican candidates who went down under straight-ticket Democratic voting.

Outside the deep South the backlash vote did not materialize. In no major city of the North or West was there a decisive defection over civil rights—not even in the industrial sections of Baltimore, Milwaukee, and Gary, Indiana, that had contributed to Governor George Wallace's successful showings in the presidential primaries. Goldwater did *not* run as well in these areas as Wallace had. New York City, Chicago, Maryland's Eastern Shore—all racial pressure points during the summer of 1964—voted Democratic in *even larger numbers* than usual.

In the North, the importance of the civil rights issue was reflected not only in the Negro vote but also in the vote of church groups in largely white communities. (One indication of this was the drop in Protestant votes for the Republican ticket from 63 percent in 1956 and 62 percent in 1960 to 45 percent for Goldwater–Miller in 1964.) Of the twenty-two northern Republican congressmen who voted against passage of the Civil Rights Act of 1964, only ten were re-elected. Twenty-one of these twenty-two suffered a reduction in their percentage of the total vote—six of the twelve who were defeated had won by 58 percent or more in 1962.

Other Issues in the 1964 Campaign:
A Round Up

DEFENSE AND FOREIGN POLICY:
THE QUESTION OF NUCLEAR RESPONSIBILITY

Public anxiety regarding the Goldwater positions on international problems cut across all the sectional and socioeconomic appeals attempted by the conservative strategists. Leading pre-election surveys showed that less than 40 percent of American voters trusted Goldwater to keep the country out of war. A great majority of the voters (60 percent) held that Goldwater was too impulsive and would shoot from the hip.

Throughout the campaign, old Goldwater positions haunted Republicans. Among them were the vote against the nuclear test-ban treaty, which an overwhelming majority of GOP senators had supported; the return to the "doctrine of brinkmanship"; the "suggestions" to defoliate Vietnamese jungles or destroy Chinese supply lines with low-yield nuclear weapons; proposals to withdraw from the United Nations if Communist China were admitted; and proposals to withdraw diplomatic recognition from the Soviet Union.

Experienced Republicans repeatedly told Goldwater *not* to press the issue of nuclear control since it involved highly sensitive national security procedures and was likely to arouse strong emotional reactions. He ignored the advice. General Eisenhower, the only Republican president who ever had to face the problem, retorted at a press conference: "I don't think we should reach conclusions telling the President what he should do or what he should say."

The Goldwater–Miller charges that President Johnson was "soft on communism" offended most American voters. Pre-election surveys indicated that an overwhelming 84 percent of American voters thought the United States should continue to negotiate with the Soviet Union on a broad front in the hope of reaching agreements that would contribute to world peace. And 72 percent favored continued negotiation with Russia toward bilateral disarmament. In a pre-election Gallup poll, only 7 percent of the voters felt communism was a major issue, although 46 percent (the largest for any issue) thought international problems were.

Public confidence in Republican foreign policy leadership reached a new low in 1964—tarnishing a distinguished tradition and jeopardizing the party's claim to future allegiance.

SOCIAL SECURITY AND MEDICAL CARE
FOR THE AGED

The Republican record on social security and medical care had for the last twelve years appealed to most voters as both realistic and forward-looking. Although social security originally had been enacted under Franklin Roosevelt, its first great expansion came under President Eisenhower in 1954, with the biggest single benefit increase in the program's history and coverage of 10 million additional workers. In the area of medical care, the Eisenhower administration's 1960 Kerr–Mills program also represented responsible Republican action.

Goldwater's record—a series of statements over the last several years in favor of making social security "voluntary" and the fact that he was *one of only two senators who voted against Kerr–Mills* —provided an inviting target for Democratic strategists.

Goldwater campaigned on his support for the 1956 amendments to the Social Security Act and his 1958 vote "to raise benefits so that their value in terms of purchasing power would be preserved." He had reversed his position on Kerr–Mills by 1963, and in 1964 accused the Democratic administration of "sabotaging" it.

The impact of these issues is suggested by the fact that the biggest switch (13 percent) among age groups from Republican to Democratic presidential votes between 1960 and 1964 occurred among voters fifty years and older. Traditional Republican appeals to senior voters (financial and social stability) were disastrously reversed. Normally conservative senior citizens gave Goldwater 20 percent fewer votes than they had given to Eisenhower in 1956.

MORALITY

The morality issue backfired in the 1964 campaign. Charges of indiscretion in the Democratic Administration, without the Republican disabilities of this campaign, could have had substantial success as they did in 1952. But the use of the morality issue became so irresponsible that American voters had little taste for it.

To be sure, Goldwater's appeal for law and order (though he never was explicit as to what he would do about the problem) in itself achieved remarkable success. Reliable surveys indicated that more voters (57 percent) trusted Goldwater's ability to maintain law and order than to handle any other problem. The irony was that they had less confidence in his handling of Negro racial problems than any other except social security. Even though Goldwater could appeal successfully to the voter's basic dissatisfaction with the present crime rate, they had little trust in his ability to solve the underlying problem he implied was an important cause of it—Negro violence. Moreover, Goldwater's pointed references to the high crime rate of Washington, D.C. (54 percent Negro population) were dulled by FBI disclosures that Phoenix, Arizona (95 percent white population) had a crime rate one-third higher than the nation's capital.

Because women ordinarily are more sensitive than men to candidates who represent stability and security, it is significant that 1964 was the first election in many years in which a smaller percentage of women (38 percent) than men (40 percent) voted Republican. In 1960, a majority (51 percent) of American women voters had cast their ballots for Nixon–Lodge; Eisenhower garnered 58 percent and 61 percent of this vote in 1952 and 1956 respectively.

ECONOMIC POLICY AND THE BUSINESS VOTE

Goldwater needed a high percentage of the business vote. He failed to gain it. His opposition to the tax cut offended many businessmen, as could have been predicted. (Henry Ford II and Stuart Saunders of the Pennsylvania Railroad had even headed a nation-wide Republican Business Committee for Tax Reduction.) Fear of abrupt change and uncertainty generated by the vagueness and inconsistency of Goldwater's programs further discredited the Senator's cause.

Meanwhile, President Johnson offered a stable and successfully functioning fiscal and monetary program. Prosperity and price stability enhanced his appeal.

The results:

1. Incredibly the percentage of professional and business defections (12 percent) from the Republican party in 1964 exceeded those of any other occupational group.
2. Even among voters with high incomes, a traditional Republican stronghold, Goldwater ran appreciably worse than Nixon had throughout the country. The Democrats made improvements over Kennedy's performance with this group ranging from about 50 percent in such states as Colorado, Michigan, Minnesota, and Ohio to an astounding 79 percent increase in California.*

LABOR ISSUES AND THE LABOR VOTE

The American labor movement organized a more intensive campaign against Goldwater than any other presidential candidate in recent history. This resistance stemmed principally from the Senator's long history of anti-labor statements and the impression that the whole thrust of his social and economic thinking was contrary to the goals of the labor movement. The Goldwater strategists mistakingly counted on the white backlash to offset their candidate's substantial deficit with labor.

Consequently:

1. Voters had less confidence in Goldwater's ability to handle the problem of labor and labor-management relations than almost any other problem (less confidence only for Negro racial problems and social security).
2. Traditionally, Republicans have held at least a strong minority of the labor vote. Indeed, in 1956, Eisenhower won 50 percent of the labor vote. Goldwater got only 29 percent. With the country's population continuing to center in metropolitan in-

---

* A *Fortune* magazine study showed that in 1964, for the first time, the Democratic party received greater financial support from businessmen than did the GOP.

dustrial areas, no amount of rural success could ever offset the kind of beating the Republicans took from labor in 1964.

3. The Goldwater backlash appeal was decisively rejected. The Republican showing in supposedly strong backlash wards was pitifully low, often under the 29 percent national average for the labor vote, as in Milwaukee, Wisconsin (16.4 percent for Goldwater) or Baltimore, Maryland (25.3 percent for Goldwater).

IMMIGRATION AND NATIONALITIES

The Goldwater–Miller–Burch strategy to win the nationalities vote was a complete failure. Rank with prejudice and highly unrealistic, it had disastrous results on election day.

The captive nations appeal had little effect on Americans of eastern European descent who were born here or who have been in this country for more than thirty years.

Moreover, the backlash appeal would have been tragic even if successful. Typical was the Republican billboard in a highly Polish area of Milwaukee, Wisconsin, urging: "Let's keep our children in our neighborhood schools. Vote Goldwater." Milwaukee Republican County Supervisor Donald F. Weber told the Milwaukee *Journal* just before the election that this kind of thinly veiled appeal to bigotry had brought him to the verge of resigning from the party.

Incredible also was the appeal by candidate William Miller who promised an audience of workers in Gary, Indiana, that the Republican party could be counted on to save jobs by not liberalizing immigration quotas. This was a complete reversal of the Eisenhower Administration's immigration policy.

The results:

1. No backlash. In predominantly Polish wards of Milwaukee, where Governor Wallace had obtained 32 percent of the vote, Goldwater won only 18 percent. Republicans similarly failed to win a majority *in any county* carried by Wallace in his presidential primaries in Maryland, Indiana, and Wisconsin.
2. Republicans were routed among all major ethnic groups. In the Irish precincts of Massachusetts, Kennedy's majority of 81 percent actually was surpassed with 88 percent by President Johnson. In the Jewish precincts of New York, California, Colorado, and Florida, Goldwater rarely obtained more than 10 percent of the vote. Johnson won overwhelming majorities of the Italian vote in all states (89 percent in Massachusetts), the Slavic vote (80 percent in Wisconsin and 88 percent in Michigan).

EXTREMISM

Extremism was a significant issue of the 1964 campaign. At the height of the campaign, a leading survey showed that 46 percent of American voters considered Goldwater "an extremist—a radical."

How did the Arizona Senator get this image? Long before the San Francisco convention, numerous right-wing extremist groups had publicly announced a Goldwater Republican candidacy as a primary objective. At the same time prominent Republican leaders such as Senators Milton Young (N.D.) and Thomas Kuchel (Calif.) issued warnings about the "hate" mail and literature discharged by some of these groups, and the right-wing takeover of local Republican organizations. The assassination of President Kennedy brought a national sense of revulsion against extremists of the right as well as those of the left. Yet Goldwater repeatedly refused to renounce the support of such right-wing extremist organizations as the John Birch Society, the Minutemen, and the Anti-Communist Christian Crusade.

In San Francisco, for the first time since 1924—when the Ku Klux Klan plagued the Democrats—extremism was a burning issue at the convention of a major party. Governor Rockefeller was harassed for condemning extremists. Not even a vaguely worded censure was accepted. Goldwater's acceptance speech—"extremism in the defense of liberty is no vice"—marked the zenith of the Senator's public association with extremism.

At the Republican unity meeting in August at Hershey, Pennsylvania, Goldwater tried to dispel fears of extremism in the campaign by declaring, "I seek the support of no extremist, of the left or of the right" and by repudiating the "character assassins, vigilantes, communists, and any group such as the Ku Klux Klan which seeks to impose its views through terror or threat or violence." It was a significant step in the right direction, but, although it may have conciliated General Eisenhower and other leaders at Hershey, it had scarcely any impact on the American voters. The damage had already been done in San Francisco.

Shortly after the nomination, former California Congressman John Rousselot, now the officer in charge of organization for the John Birch Society, proclaimed that over 100 delegates and alternates to the Convention were members of the Society.

Despite Goldwater's assurance in Hershey that he would seek no extremist support, the assistance of right-wing groups was tacitly—and often openly—used and appreciated by the Goldwater organization. Right-wing books were donated to and sold by Goldwater's

Phoenix headquarters, with the proceeds used to help meet campaign expenses.

Post-election surveys have indicated that a major concern of many Republican leaders in all parts of the country is the party's residual extremist image. Unless this identification of the Republican party with the far right is erased the Democrats will run against extremist-republicanism in the future just as successfully as they ran against "Hoovervilles" for decades after the depression.

And Around the Country

THE BIG CITIES

Goldwater's opposition to bills providing federal aid in such fields as urban mass transportation, anti-poverty programs, higher education, expanded vocational education, air pollution, combined with other issues to further weaken the Republican position in urban areas.

In all parts of the country, Goldwater did worse than Nixon in the big cities, reflecting the utter failure to heed Senator Thruston Morton's admonition that the Kennedy–Nixon contest was lost in the ten largest cities. In the big city precincts of the North the Republican vote fell from 38 percent to 26 percent—in the West it dropped from 48 percent to 39 percent.

THE SUBURBS

Wherever the "silent" conservative vote was supposed to appear on election day, 1964, suburbia must not have been the place. The Democrats established more beachheads in the American suburbs than in any other election in recent memory.

Many famous suburbs of the country—Westchester, Wellesley, Chestnut Hill—had not gone Democrat in fifty-two years. They did in 1964. In New York, President Johnson carried once bedrock-Republican Nassau, Suffolk, and Westchester counties by astounding margins. County courthouses in these suburbs were also lost. In New York and New Jersey, the President swept every county, something that has never happened before; in Wisconsin all but three counties; in Michigan all but two.

In the suburbs of Boston, Goldwater ran 20 percent behind Nixon; in Buffalo 17 percent; in Denver 17 percent; in Detroit 14 percent. The calamity in the suburbs carried over directly to Republican seats in Congress. Of the fifty congressional seats classified by *Congressional Quarterly* as suburban in character, Republican holdings went from thirty-one to twenty-six—nearly all losses coming in "safe" GOP districts. Once considered the most promising area for Republican growth, the suburbs in 1964 were sacrificed for the southern strategy. It will require intensive effort to regain them in 1966 and 1968.

FARM PROBLEMS AND THE FARM VOTE

The 1964 election was a disaster in the traditionally Republican farm belt. The Republican presidential ticket failed to carry a single midwestern farm state—and it dragged to defeat hundreds of state and local candidates. The reversal was most drastic in Iowa where the Democrats gained control of most major offices.

Goldwater had pledged that "it is the goal of the Republican party that there be a free and prosperous American agriculture with a minimum of federal controls and interference." The major failing was that the Goldwater–Miller strategists never explained how federal interference was to be reduced. Farmers worried about the transition period and the fate of the small farmer. Pre-election surveys showed that voters had no greater confidence in Goldwater's ability to handle agricultural problems than to keep the country out of war.

The Democratic farm record was vulnerable in many ways, but the Republicans never exploited this weakness. Surveys indicated that the nationally dominant issues of nuclear responsibility, social security, and, to a lesser extent, civil rights were more significant to a large number of farmers than the farm problem itself.

On election day, not only was there no "silent conservative" vote in the farm states, but the Republican party suffered a calamity. With just 47 percent of the vote, the GOP became the minority party among farmers for the first time since World War II.

U.S. News & World Report surveyed 334 townships where farm population is 75 percent or more of the total. In 74 Iowa townships in the corn, hog, and cash-grain belt, Johnson ran 14 percent ahead of Kennedy's vote; in 31 similar townships in Indiana, the Democratic total was 12 percent above 1960. In the dairy area of Southeast Minnesota, 153 townships gave Goldwater 16 percent fewer votes than they gave Nixon; and in 76 townships in the wheat and cattle area of Western Kansas, the 1964 GOP vote was 12 percent lower than in 1960.

Although Goldwater generally ran 16 percent behind Nixon's performance in the rural precincts of the North and West, he did manage to gain slightly in the rural South.

YOUTH

Historians of the future may well record that the most significant result of the 1964 election was that America's youth turned against the Republican party. A carefully conducted survey among college students by the Gallup poll showed that Johnson was preferred over Goldwater by more than two to one. Moreover, an audit of campus mock elections showed that Johnson won from 52 to 93 percent of the total vote. He even carried a mock election at the University of Arizona.

The actual election results among the youngest generation of voters—the 21–29 age group—demonstrates the seriousness of the problem. The Republican presidential ticket won only 36 percent of this future leadership group in 1964, a sharp drop (10 percent) from Nixon's performance against Kennedy.

The situation is particularly ironic since Senator Goldwater counted the nation's youth as his most sympathetic audience. College students respected him even though he had voted against virtually all federal school grant programs and the 1958 National Defense Education Act. And there are indications that Goldwater's tax credit proposals for financing education could have had successful appeal to youth. But their support for Goldwater diminished as his positions on civil rights, foreign policy, and extremism broke sharply with the postwar generation's concept of America's future.

Conclusion

Issues were critical in the 1964 campaign. Goldwater found himself on the wrong side of many of them when he left San Francisco. His campaign forfeited whatever issues were left. His opponents attacked his past record and then charged him with inconsistency when he retreated from it. In all, the Goldwater campaign revealed that merely taking a stand on issues is not nearly enough. The voters expect of their leaders not only *conscience*, but a *consciousness* of the nation's needs and goals. In this light, the outcome of Election '64 was all too predictable.

3

Thе Results:

"Reaping the Whirlwind"

It is not often that careful students of American politics talk seriously about the possible demise of a major party. But such talk echoed from one end of the country to another during the last two months of 1964—so great was the extent of the Republican disaster. Never—since it had been founded in 1854 —had the "Grand Old Party" been closer to collapse.

For it was not only the presidential candidate who was rejected in 1964. The Goldwater undertow swamped the Republican cause in local, state, and congressional elections. Many observed that the voters showed an unprecedented ferocity in voting against Goldwater. The intensity of their feeling could not be vented by pulling a single lever or marking a single box. And so they went down the ticket—carefully rejecting those candidates who had associated themselves with Goldwater and supporting those who had not. More than one candidate breathed a sigh of relief when he learned that Goldwater or Miller would not be able to appear with him during the campaign.

The voters wanted no part of right-wing Republicans throughout 1964. Goldwater trailed other Republicans in every pre-convention poll. In late July, Gallup showed Goldwater 31 percent, Johnson 62 percent, undecided 7 percent. By election eve it was Goldwater 32 percent, Johnson 61 percent, undecided 7 percent. The actual results were Goldwater 38.7 percent, Johnson 61.3 percent. And yet *The National Review* had assured conservatives in July:

> Already the pollsters are predicting a bloodcurdling defeat for Goldwater in November. Let us remember their ignorance, their ineptitude, their sublime wrongheadedness in March, April, and May and not be dismayed.

They should have been dismayed. Consider these facts: President Johnson—certainly not the most popular man ever to seek the presidency—set an all time record by polling almost sixteen million

45

votes more than his opponent. President Kennedy's margin in 1960 was only 112,803. Johnson's was 140 times as large.

Johnson won 44 states, 36 of them by over 55 percent of the vote—the traditional test of a landslide margin. Goldwater thought in January that he would get at least 45 percent nationally. Yet, outside the South, only five states (Utah, Nebraska, Kansas, Idaho and his home state of Arizona) gave Goldwater 45 percent or more. If he could have magically obtained the electoral vote of every state in which he polled even 45 percent he would *still* have been overwhelmingly beaten: 444 to 94.

Goldwater set an all time record by losing six states by more than a million votes: New York—where he lost by more than two million—Pennsylvania, Michigan, Ohio, Massachusetts, and California. All of these states have recently shown an inclination to vote Republican. All but California presently have Republican Governors —all but Michigan have at least one Republican Senator.

Most significantly, Goldwater carried only sixty congressional districts and *only sixteen* of them were outside the South. Six of these were in Southern California, five in suburban Chicago, and one each in Arizona, Kentucky, Idaho, Nebraska, and Oklahoma. He did not carry one congressional district anywhere else! Contrast this with 1960, when Nixon beat Kennedy in congressional districts, 228 to 206. Moreover, of the 228 Nixon districts, Goldwater let 201 slip away. He held on to only twenty-seven of them— and in twenty of these he ran behind the Nixon pace. He did add thirty new districts that Nixon did not carry—all of them in the South.

GOP candidates for president invariably run ahead of the party's congressional candidates. Nixon, for example, ran ahead in 311 congressional districts in 1960. In 1964, Goldwater ran ahead of Republican congressional candidates in only 161 districts—ninety-five of them in the South. But even in these limited areas, Goldwater's coattails were the weakest in American political history. Nixon had pulled to victory several dozen of the congressional candidates whose vote totals trailed his. Of the congressional candidates who ran behind Goldwater, only seven won—five in Alabama, one each in Mississippi and Georgia. He was able to pull no Senate or gubernatorial candidate to victory.

Election Results in Congress

In the Senate elections the Republicans suffered a net loss of two seats in 1964. With a moderate national ticket the Republicans could have shown a net gain of five seats in the Senate. The weakness of the Goldwater–Miller ticket was directly responsible for the loss of two Senate seats (in New Mexico and New York). The weakness of the national ticket also prevented Republican candidates from winning five new Senate seats (in Nevada, Ohio, Oklahoma, Wisconsin, and Wyoming).

In the House of Representatives the Republicans suffered a net loss of thirty-eight seats in 1964. With a moderate national ticket the Republicans could have shown a net gain of eleven seats in the House of Representatives. The loss of forty-two Republican seats is directly attributable to the Goldwater–Miller ticket (which also produced the election of seven new Republicans in the South). Furthermore, the weakness of the Republican national ticket deprived the Republican party of thirteen new seats in Democratic districts.

Following the 1962 elections, the Republican National Committee under Chairman Miller classified as "marginal" thirty-eight seats held by Democrats and thirty-seven seats held by Republicans. A district is commonly considered to be marginal if it had been won with less than 55 percent of the votes in the previous election. In 1964, of the thirty-eight marginal seats held by Democrats, Republicans won only two (in California and Idaho). Of the thirty-seven marginal seats held by Republicans, Democrats captured eighteen.

But of greatest significance is the fact that Goldwater's candidacy failed in large part to help even those whom it purported to aid most, namely conservative Republicans. On June 17, 1964, fifty-four Republican congressmen endorsed Senator Goldwater, saying: "We are convinced that the nomination of Senator Barry Goldwater will result in substantial increases in Republican membership in both houses of Congress." Of this group, seventeen (one-third) were defeated, twenty-five suffered reductions in their winning percentages as compared to the 1962 elections, five retired, and only seven improved upon their performances in the previous election—four of them southerners.

It is most interesting to note the average ACA rating (an index to conservative voting patterns) for the thirty-six incumbent Republican congressmen who were defeated was 80.6 percent. The Goldwater campaign cannot be said to have helped the conservative cause.

At the State Level

Like the party in Congress, the Republican party in the states went into the election holding a distinct minority of state elective offices. Republicans occupied only 40 percent of the state legislative seats and less than one-third of the governorships in the country prior to the 1964 election. With a large number of Democratic seats thus up for election, the GOP had an opportunity to make important gains, continuing the marked upward trend since the setback of 1958.

The Republicans in 1964 showed a net gain of one governorship. With a moderate national ticket the party could have had a net gain of six governorships. Of the two losses (in Arizona and Utah), neither could have been prevented with a more moderate national ticket. Similarly, the three new Republican governorships (in Massachusetts, Washington, and Wisconsin) were won in spite of, not because of, the Goldwater–Miller ticket. However, the weakness of the national ticket deprived the Republican party of five new governorships (in Delaware, Illinois, Indiana, North Carolina, and West Virginia). GOP gains in the state legislatures that had been steadily built up over the past six years were totally wiped out in 1964. In six states the Republicans lost control of both houses of the state legislature.

Before the election, Republicans had controlled both houses in nineteen state legislatures, the Democrats, twenty-five. After the Goldwater debacle, the Republicans controlled both houses in only seven. The GOP lost control of fourteen lower houses and seven upper houses. It said good-by to ninety upper house seats and almost 450 lower house seats in the state legislatures. The party is now once again as weak in the states as it was during the depression.

The 27,000,000

Despite the great damage suffered by the GOP in 1964, Goldwater partisans have unstintingly contended that the 27,000,000 people who voted for Goldwater represent an enormous tide of conservative sentiment in the country. The argument that those 27,000,000 are all undeviating conservatives and adherents of Goldwaterism is supported by neither the test of reason nor the test of statistics.

Noted pollster Louis Harris reported on January 11, 1965, that— on the basis of extensive interviews and other election data—"only approximately 6 million of the 27 million who voted for the Goldwater–Miller ticket can be considered hard-core, down-the-line Goldwater supporters." He pointed out that eighteen million voted for the Republican nominee "primarily because of party loyalty" while expressing serious reservations about his policies. Another three million—including two million southern Democrats—were motivated mainly by the race issue.

Moreover, a *majority* of those who voted *for* Goldwater classified themselves as moderate or liberal in political philosophy! And even the minority of Goldwater voters who called themselves conservatives were not all Barry-men. Over one-third (36 percent) of them described Goldwater as more of a radical than a conservative. *A clear majority of the twenty-seven million Goldwater voters opposed a right-wing takeover of the Republican party.* *

Late in December, *The New York Times* had reported on a nationwide survey that showed that over 60 percent of the Goldwater voters thought that the Arizona Senator should be replaced as party leader; that less than 20 percent—or approximately 5.4 million voters—thought he should be retained. Local polls produced similar results. Only 11 percent of the Minnesotans who voted for Goldwater thought that he should be nominated again. Of these supporters, 73 percent thought that another Republican candidate would have done better.**

In March of 1965, a further study by pollster Louis H. Bean and columnist Roscoe Drummond awarded Goldwater even less hardline support. It concluded that "the pure Goldwater vote lies between 2,500,000 and 3,000,000—not more." The rest of the 27 million "is the party vote." Meanwhile the Gallup poll showed that only 15 percent of the 1964 GOP voters considered Goldwater the party's most representative candidate.†

The election statistics themselves show that many Goldwater voters also cast votes for liberal candidates in state races. In Montana, for example, Goldwater ran 5.2 percent ahead of the GOP candidate for Senator, indicating a sizeable swing of Goldwater voters to Senator Mike Mansfield, Democratic Majority Leader in the Senate. The same phenomenon occurred in Washington, where Goldwater ran almost 10 percent ahead of the Senate candidate, revealing a large shift of Goldwater voters to Senator Henry Jackson—former Democratic National Chairman. In John Lindsay's district (New York's 17th) Goldwater received 37 percent of the vote while the same electorate was giving 71 percent to Lindsay and—most significantly—only 5 percent to Lindsay's *Conservative* party opponent. The gubernatorial contests in Iowa and Nebraska show the same pattern. Obviously, it cannot be maintained that all 27 million people who voted for Goldwater are steadfast conservatives of the Goldwater type.

As the surveys indicate, many different kinds of voters con-

---

* "Few Real Barrymen," a survey report by Louis Harris as reported in *The Boston Globe*, January 11, 1965 p. 7.

** *The New York Times*, December 18, 1964, p. 1; *Minneapolis Tribune*, December 20, 1964.

† Louis H. Bean and Roscoe Drummond, "How Many Votes does Goldwater Own?" *Look*, March 23, 1965, pp. 75–76.

tributed to the Goldwater–Miller total. Most were rock-ribbed Republicans who regarded the election in partisan rather than philosophical terms and who always vote for the GOP candidate without regard to ideology. Many Goldwater voters were merely dissatisfied with the party in power or with its candidate, but would not consider themselves implacable conservatives. Many were not conservatives at all. As is true in any national election, the votes on both sides reflected a coalition of feelings on great and small issues and were not divisible in a liberal–conservative polarity.

TABLE 1. Percentage of Vote by Groups in Presidential Elections—1952–1964*

	1952		1956		1960		1964		Net Shift, 1960-1964	
	D %	R %	D %	R %	D %	R %	D %	R %	D %	R %
National	44.6	55.4	42.2	57.8	50.1	49.9	61.3	38.7	+11.2	−11.2
Men	47	53	45	55	52	48	60	40	+ 8	− 8
Women	42	58	39	61	49	51	62	38	+13	−13
White	43	57	41	59	49	51	59	41	+10	−10
Nonwhite	79	21	61	39	68	32	94	6	+26	−26
College	34	66	31	69	39	61	52	48	+13	−13
High School	45	55	42	58	52	48	62	38	+10	−10
Grade School	52	48	50	50	55	45	66	34	+11	−11
Prof. & Bus.	36	64	32	68	42	58	54	46	+12	−12
White Collar	40	60	37	63	48	52	57	43	+ 9	− 9
Manual	55	45	50	50	60	40	71	29	+11	−11
Farmers	33	67	46	54	48	52	53	47	+ 5	− 5
21–29 yrs.	51	49	43	57	54	46	64	36	+10	−10
30–49 yrs.	47	53	45	55	54	46	63	37	+ 9	− 9
50 yrs. & older	39	61	39	61	46	54	59	41	+13	−13
Protestant	37	63	37	63	38	62	55	45	+17	−17
Catholic	56	44	51	49	78	22	76	24	− 2	+ 2
Republicans	8	92	4	96	5	95	20	80	+15	−15
Democrats	77	23	85	15	84	16	87	13	+ 3	− 3
Independents	35	65	30	70	43	57	56	44	+13	−13
East	45	55	40	60	53	47	68	32	+15	−15
Midwest	42	58	41	59	48	52	61	39	+13	−13
South	51	49	49	51	51	49	52	48	+ 1	− 1
West	42	58	43	57	49	51	60	40	+11	−11

* Estimated from national survey by the Gallup Poll.
SOURCE: The Gallup Poll as reproduced in *The Congressional Quarterly*, Dec. 25, 1964.

What Happened on November 3?
*A Region-by-Region Analysis**

We present now a region-by-region picture of the election results in 1964. For Republicans—and for all Americans who are concerned about the health of the two-party system—it is not a very pretty story. We tell it again because we are too well aware of the truth of the dictum, "Those who do not remember the past are condemned to repeat it."

NEW ENGLAND

In traditionally Republican New England, the Goldwater candidacy was a total disaster. Republican Governor John Reed summed up the story in *Maine:* "A Democratic tidal wave hit our rock-bound coast in proportions never before experienced. . . . I am convinced that the primary reason for the outcome can be traced squarely to the unacceptance of the Republican National ticket in my state." The results supported his conclusion: The GOP Senate candidate, Clifford McIntire, and the one congressional candidate who supported Goldwater were badly beaten.

The other congressional candidate, Congressman Stanley Tupper, was not. Tupper was an incumbent who had served as New England coordinator for the Rockefeller presidential campaign. During the campaign, he went so far as to say in a televised broadcast that he would not vote for Goldwater. His well-known stand caused many Goldwater Republicans to disown him. Over 25 percent of those voters who otherwise cast a straight Republican ballot did not vote for Tupper. Nevertheless, he won a narrow victory against overwhelming odds. Tupper's win has meant increased influence for him within the state organization; the state committee finally even granted him $1000 to help defray costs of the vote recount.

Most dramatic was the effect of the Goldwater–Miller blight on the state legislature. Both houses had been in Republican control since the First World War. Both were lost in 1964. Before the election there were twenty-nine Republicans and five Democrats in the state Senate. After the election there were twenty-nine Democrats and five Republicans! A sixty-nine-seat plurality was wiped out in the lower house.

---

* This material is adapted from the original Ripon Society analysis, *Election '64*, which contained a state by state discussion of the election results. Copies of *Election '64* may be obtained through the Ripon Society office, Box 138, Cambridge, Mass. 02138.

Striking was the amount of straight ticket Democratic voting. In one Saco ward, where only 1800 Democrats are registered, there were 2400 *straight* Democratic ballots cast. One Republican woman voter explained what happened in Maine most precisely. She and many others, she said, wanted to "wipe out the entire slate so we can start fresh the next time."

The story in *New Hampshire* was similar. The congressional incumbent who backed Goldwater was a victim of the national ticket and the one who remained somewhat distant survived. The Democratic Governor was re-elected by better than two to one. Democrats scored gains in both houses of the legislature though the GOP retained shaky control of both. New Hampshire is one of only seven states where this is true.

In *Vermont* the lesson of the Goldwater undertow was demonstrated more clearly than anywhere else. In a state that had *never* gone Democratic in a presidential race, Johnson got almost twice as many votes as Goldwater. Under a system of multiple ballots, state officers appear on the ballot with the presidential contest. Democrats swept all of them. A separate ballot lists Senate and congressional races. Here the Republicans won. Senator Prouty explained his victory this way: "I won because I presented a positive program for educating the young and aiding the elderly. The Republican party will become the majority party only when voters know what it is for as well as what it is against." Able and moderate, Congressman Robert Stafford also took his contest in stride.

But in the state offices, the story was far different. Democratic candidates were incredulous when they learned that the Vermont voters had put them in office. The Attorney-General elect said, "I was interested in the job, but I didn't think I had a chance, so rather than wage a half-hearted campaign, I waged no campaign at all. I was simply startled beyond belief. You know, I just got on the ticket to fill the ballot." Also startled by their election were the eighty-one and seventy-one year old Democratic candidates for Treasurer and Secretary of the state. In the State Senate Republicans lost four seats. For the first time in memory, the Democrats held over 40 percent of the seats. Yet, in 1965, reapportionment elections were a different story. Relieved of the Goldwater albatross, Vermont Republicans made an overwhelming comeback, winning both houses with over 75 percent of the seats. Democratic Governor Phillip H. Hoff lamented, "We took a terrible drubbing."

On the southern New England tier, things were even worse in 1964. Johnson got 76 percent of the vote in *Massachusetts*—even edging Senator Edward Kennedy who picked up 75 percent. The Democratic Secretary of State Kevin White got 70 percent. But

Massachusetts voters proved their independence and their ability to make distinctions. For they also elected former Republican Governor John Volpe, a new Republican Lieutenant Governor, Elliot Richardson—and, most encouragingly, Negro Republican Attorney General Edward Brooke. All overcame the 1,200,000 Goldwater deficit, with Brooke establishing a national record for split-ticket voting when he won by 800,000 votes. This meant that over a million Johnson voters split their tickets to vote for Brooke.

Nevertheless, the Republican organization grows weaker and weaker in Massachusetts. In the lower house of the state legislature, the GOP lost twenty-one seats from what was thought to have been rock bottom. The party will have difficulty surviving another presidential candidate who can get no more than 25 percent of the Massachusetts vote.

In *Rhode Island,* the Democratic percentage was the highest of any state. Goldwater got only 19 percent of the vote, in a state where General Eisenhower had won 58.4 percent in 1956. Republican Governor John Chafee, who had strenuously opposed Goldwater's nomination, was re-elected by a margin greater than Goldwater's total vote in Rhode Island! In the face of the Johnson landslide, Chafee still won by more than 85,000 votes. The popular Governor sought to maintain an image of independence. He alone survived the Democratic blitz, partly because his campaign included education in split-ticket voting.

GOP House and Senate candidates were badly beaten, and Republican strength in the state legislature dwindled. Chafee's post-election comment read this lesson from the disaster: "I think the Party will probably be molded in a more liberal way of thinking."

In *Connecticut,* the Republican appeal had been in decline since the 1950s. Goldwater destroyed its remaining bastions—most of them in the suburbs and small towns. For the first time West Hartford went Democratic—by almost two to one. Johnson carried Fairfield County by almost 70,000 votes.

The Goldwater candidacy cost the Republicans a potenial gain in one congressional district, and an incumbent in another—the popular and moderate Abner W. Sibal. Sibal ran an astounding 20,000 votes ahead of Goldwater. Moderates have rallied their forces since 1964, but remain under constant harassment from the right wing. Goldwater strategist John Lupton heads his own independent political organization—and has successfully sought outside support from national figures like George Murphy and Ronald Reagan. Lupton commented immediately after the election on some of the non-Goldwater Republicans who are active in the regular party: "We're going to knock them off, one by one."

MIDDLE ATLANTIC STATES

In *New York,* Goldwater did to the Republican party exactly what it was expected he would do—he defeated them far more effectively than their Democratic opponents could have done unaided. The state GOP lost a Senate seat, seven House seats, and both branches of the state legislature—for the first time since 1935. Goldwater had no important sources of strength in the state and he never attempted to cultivate any. Indifference of local organizations undoubtedly contributed to the defeat. This indifference was born of many factors, most importantly the uncooperative attitude of the National Committee during the campaign. One county chairman said in October, "We just can't get to those people. They won't talk to us and they won't listen. I've never seen such a terrible campaign." As a result, the local organizations increasingly turned their attention to the local races. Goldwater lost every one of the state's sixty-two counties, the first time in history that this has happened. In William Miller's home congressional district, the Republican ticket failed to get even one-third of the vote.

Senator Kenneth B. Keating's re-election campaign suffered from some strategic errors—particularly regarding a proposed debate with his opponent. Yet, it can be argued that Robert Kennedy rode into office on Lyndon Johnson's coattails. Goldwater's losing margin was 1,750,000 votes larger than Keating's.

Six of the seven congressional losses were conservative incumbent congressmen running for re-election. The most notable Republican victories were those of congressmen like Halpern, Lindsay, and Reid who avoided identification with Goldwater. Congressman Lindsay achieved a spectacular victory (71 percent) against two opponents—a Democrat and a Goldwater organizer who ran as a Conservative party candidate.

The GOP lost control of both Houses of the Legislature. The decline was marked by the personal defeat of the Republican delegation. One defeated candidate was David Weiner, who had publicly made his peace with Goldwater after the San Francisco convention, and Senator Walter Mahoney, a veteran from upstate.

The Johnson plurality in *New Jersey* was forty-one times as large as Kennedy's sizable victory margin in 1960. The President carried all twenty-one counties, as Eisenhower had done in 1956. (Even F.D.R. had carried only seventeen in 1936). Just before the election, Dean Burch had hinted that he had expected a stunning upset in New Jersey. But Goldwater carried only 34 percent of the vote and caused the defeat of four incumbent congressmen.

This is the first time since Woodrow Wilson's triumph in 1912 that the Democrats have controlled the New Jersey congressional delegation. One defeated candidate was David Weiner, who had fought to distinguish his moderate views from Goldwater's: "My election was lost in the Cow Palace in San Francisco," he observed. "Goldwater lost my district by 49,500 while I lost by 11,000."

Fortunately for Republicans there was no contest for the State Legislature in 1964.

Unprecedented ticket-splitting enabled *Pennsylvania* Republicans to limit the effect of the Goldwater catastrophe. Most significant was the hard-earned victory of Senator Hugh Scott. While the national ticket lost sixty-one of Pennsylvania's sixty-seven counties, Scott captured forty-four. He ran more than 600,000 votes ahead of Goldwater. In Philadelphia he cut significantly into the Negro vote. Goldwater lost Philadelphia by 400,000 votes, a record margin that clearly rejected any hint of a backlash. L.B.J. carried GOP strongholds like Bucks and Montgomery counties; Scott took both of these as well.

Pennsylvania ticket-splitters also saved several congressional candidates, but the Goldwater undertow did cost the GOP two congressmen. The national ticket ran 417,000 votes behind the total votes cast for GOP congressional candidates. Contrast this with 1960, when Richard Nixon received 44,000 votes more than the congressional total and with 1956 when President Eisenhower ran almost 200,000 votes ahead.

On the morning after the election, veteran reporter Ned Davis of the Wilmington *Morning News* summarized the political story in *Delaware*: "The results show that Delaware Republicans were deprived of victory by the decided unpopularity of Senator Goldwater. It was obvious that the President pulled [Charles W.] Terry (Democratic candidate for governor) and many other candidates, both statewide and in the county and legislative races, to triumph with him."

Johnson's Delaware victory, although by the smallest percentage in the East, 61 percent, was the widest margin given to a presidential candidate since 1928. More important for the future were the trends in registration. In Wilmington, the Democrats outscored the Republicans by almost five to one among new voters. In strong GOP areas, registration still ran from 50 percent to 70 percent Democratic. Only popular Senator John J. Williams could swim against the tide.

THE BORDER STATES

Senator Goldwater had reason to be optimistic about *Maryland*. Alabama's Governor George Wallace had received 43 percent of the vote in the May Democratic primary. Republicans had recently won in the state, having held the governorship, both Senate seats and several congressional spots at various times over the past ten years. But President Johnson established a new state record in 1964 by winning 65.5 percent of the vote. He carried twenty-one of the state's twenty-five counties (Kennedy had carried only seven). Johnson even came close to carrying the racially torn eastern shore—despite predictions of significant white backlash and overwhelming Goldwater strength.

The Democratic landslide produced the almost two-to-one victory of Joseph Tydings over incumbent Republican Senator J. Glenn Beall. This would have been a marginal race in normal circumstances, but the Goldwater candidacy was the clincher. There was no change in the congressional lineup, though the majorities of incumbent Republicans Rogers C. B. Morton and Charles McC. Mathias were reduced. Mathias, a leading Republican moderate in the House whom Goldwater supporters had tried to dump in the May primary, defeated a strong opponent in a district in which the Democrats hold a seven-to-five registration lead and in which new registrations were running 70 percent Democratic. In the other six congressional races, GOP showings were among the worst ever.

As in the other border states, 1964 may have marked the end of hopes for a true Republican breakthrough in Maryland. Democratic registration gains were overwhelming. In some Negro precincts in Baltimore, they ran sixteen to one Democratic. This may also spell the destruction of the Negro-Republican alliance which was so carefully nourished by former Republican Governor and now Baltimore Mayor Theodore McKeldin as the formula for GOP victory.

In 1964, the residents of the *District of Columbia* cast votes for the presidency for the first time in the District's history. They went for Johnson eight to one (85.5 percent). D.C. Republican Chairman Carl Shipley exclaimed: "We were not only defeated, we were also slaughtered by as much as 300 to 1 in some precincts." All this despite the fact that—until this year—Republican sentiment had been strong among Negroes in the District.

In *West Virginia,* "everyone votes their belly," and the Republican outlook was never bright. But scandals and good GOP candidates promised some gains in 1964. Most observers predicted a 100,000 vote margin for President Johnson; he actually won by 284,000 votes. Most observers thought popular former Republican Governor Cecil H. Underwood would be elected governor; he lost by 71,000 votes—a direct casualty of the national ticket. The Senate candidate lost, and so did several GOP incumbents in the already heavily Democratic state legislature.

The same thing happened in *Kentucky* where bold Democrats predicted an 80,000 plurality and timid ones talked about losing the state. Nobody dreamed that the actual Johnson margin would approach 300,000 of the 1,000,000 votes cast. But it did. The TVA issue hurt Goldwater badly.

A congressional seat was lost in Louisville due to the national ticket—and partially as a result of Negro support for the Democrat. The sole GOP position on the Kentucky Court of Appeals also went down the drain. In the solidly Republican rural mountain areas of the east, the Democrats made significant gains. All of this came at the expense of one of the strongest Republican state organizations ever developed in the Blue Grass state. The state chairman drew this conclusion: "I'm a conservative, but I'm willing to give a little to win sometime. You can't do anything if you don't win."

Tennessee was an ideal laboratory for testing the conservatives' southern strategy. In the east lies a strong, rural Republican region which was expected to embrace wholeheartedly the major tenets of the conservative philosophy. In the west is a Democratic region of considerable segregationist sentiment; wholesale defections to the Republicans were expected. On top of this, the Republicans had carried Tennessee for the past three Presidential elections. What better conditions for a Goldwater candidacy?

Yet, President Johnson carried Tennessee by a comfortable margin of over 125,000 votes. Goldwater trailed the rest of the Republican ticket almost everywhere. The southern strategy failed and seriously retarded the drive to make Tennessee a genuine two-party state.

It goes without saying that Goldwater's talk about selling TVA hurt him substantially. But so did his position on civil rights. Look at Shelby County, which includes Memphis, the state's largest city, where Negroes make up almost 40 percent of the population. Kennedy narrowly lost the county in 1960; Johnson carried it by 12,000 votes. The Negro vote had been decisive.

Nixon had carried the conservative eastern districts by 121,000 votes in 1960. Goldwater won by under 4,000 while all three Republican congressional candidates in the area won handily. Judging from the congressional vote, at least 75,000 Republicans in this conservative region crossed over to vote against Senator Goldwater while supporting the rest of the GOP ticket.

Two Democratic senators were elected in Tennessee, liberal Ross Bass and incumbent Albert Gore, who picked up a large part of the Negro vote *despite* his vote against the Civil Rights Act. The reason may have been that his opponent, Dan Kuykendall, had been one who helped exclude Negroes for the first time in fifty years from the Tennessee convention delegation to San Francisco. Republicans lost a chance to gain one congressional seat in the 9th District when the Democratic candidate took 99 percent of the Negro vote and only 21 percent of the white vote—enough to win a 10,000 vote plurality.

A similar pattern was evident in *Missouri,* where President Johnson developed a tremendous majority by winning heavily industrial areas, farm regions, and Negro districts. In 1960, Nixon carried rural Missouri by over 150,000 votes. In 1964, Johnson carried these same areas by over 155,000 votes. Senator Symington led the Democratic ticket with a record plurality of more than a half-million votes. Outstanding educator, Ethan Shepley, running for Governor, led the Republican ticket but lost by more than 400,000 votes. Expectations of a stronger Shepley showing were submerged in the undertow. The Democratic majority in the lower house of the state legislature added twenty-three seats to their control.

Reactions to defeat varied. Said one county chairman: "Let's put the blame where it belongs—on that bunch of cutthroats in the East, namely Rockefeller, Scranton, Lodge, Keating, and the others who worked against the Republican party." On the other hand Milton Shaw, chairman of the St. Louis Republican party, put it this way: "With another candidate for President—a more moderate candidate—I think we could have done much better."

Oklahoma is another state that, despite the four-to-one Democratic registration, has given support to Republican presidential tickets in the past. It went for Eisenhower in 1952 and 1956 and gave Nixon an overwhelming victory in 1960. It elected a GOP Governor in 1962. But in 1964 Goldwater and Miller were badly defeated and they pulled to defeat former Oklahoma University football coach Bud Wilkinson, a candidate for the U.S. Senate. Wilkinson lost by less than 25,000 votes while Goldwater lost by over 107,000. A true conservative, Wilkinson nevertheless ran an increasingly independent campaign as election day approached. But it was not independent enough. The Republican party in Oklahoma may well have learned what Bud Wilkinson had known for a long time—no matter how promising the halfback, nobody on the team wins without a strong front line.

THE SOUTH

If Senator Goldwater's southern strategy was to work anywhere it had to work in *Virginia,* which had not voted for the Democratic nominee since 1948. But the Republicans were beaten in Virginia by those new forces of southern politics which the strategy of the national ticket repeatedly ignored. The most important factor was the ability of Negroes and many whites to vote in federal elections without having to pay the cumulative poll tax. Negro registration climbed from 78,000 in 1960 to over 200,000 in 1964, and was well over 90 percent Democratic.

Furthermore, President Johnson carried the 10th Congressional District (Alexandria and Arlington) by almost two to one. This is an area of exploding population, containing many transients and non-native Virginians. The Johnson–Humphrey ticket received organizational support from associates of Senator Harry Byrd (although Byrd himself maintained his traditional silence), from the academic community, and from many business leaders and professional men who had been Republicans in the past.

Senator Byrd was re-elected, 589,000 to 170,000. Republican candidate Richard May was never publicly endorsed by the national ticket, while Goldwater awaited an endorsement from Byrd, and prominent Goldwater supporters organized Virginia Republicans for Byrd. No congressional seats changed hands, but Republican margins were cut seriously. Veteran Joel T. Broyhill himself attributed the narrowness of his margin (only 2000 votes) to the Johnson landslide in his district.

But the Virginia GOP moves ahead. Republican National Committeewoman Hazel K. Barger's comment was: "This is not the end of anything except Mr. Goldwater." State Chairman Robert Corber said: "Senator Goldwater has been completely repudiated at the polls. He should not be the leader of the party under any circumstances." Corber has since instituted a purge of Birch Society members from party committees and candidacies—with mixed success. But the GOP has begun to seek out Negro voters, and in the 1965 Governor's race, it fielded a most attractive and capable moderate candidate, Linwood Holton.

Goldwater's deficit in *North Carolina* (175,000) was three times that of Nixon in 1960. The painstaking gains of a decade were wiped out. Moderate Robert Gavin lost the Governor's race to a segregationist who nevertheless received 97 percent of the Negro vote. In addition, many GOP leaders concentrated on Goldwater and ignored Gavin. Birch Society Republicans boycotted the gubernatorial candidate. He was clearly a casualty of the national ticket as were several members of the state legislature.

State Chairman J. Herman Saxon looked at the Negro vote and said: "I definitely think we must mold on a progressive, conservative basis. What got us was that Goldwater was not a politician."

In *South Carolina,* Goldwater won and the Republican party lost. Of fifty-eight offices which Republicans contested (including two congressional seats) in thirteen of the forty-six counties, only one went for the GOP. Senator Strom Thurmond and Congressman

Albert Watson became Republicans by conversion—and while they may have temporarily aided the party in their state, the welcome they received has tarnished the party image nationally.

Of the five deep southern states that were carried by the Goldwater–Miller ticket, *Georgia*—which had never gone Republican before—best illustrates the hard choices that southern Republicans now face. The race issue was the key to victory here—as elsewhere. Success came in areas like Seminole county in the southwestern corner of the state. It went 95.4 percent for Kennedy–Johnson in 1960 but produced a 75 percent vote for Goldwater. *The Atlanta Constitution* observed "one shocking piece of evidence: the fantastic correlation between the counties former Governor Marvin Griffen (a rabid segregationist) carried, and those which Goldwater won. The significance of this is that Goldwater looked like a 'clean segregationist' to south Georgians."

But Goldwater lost votes that Nixon had received in 1960, chiefly in growing urban areas like Atlanta and, of course, among Negroes who had once been attached to the state GOP when it was under the leadership of men like Robert Snodgrass. During the campaign Snodgrass challenged the new look which his party had taken on: "The Republican Party of Georgia cannot afford—and it must not be led by—hatemongers like the Ku Kluxers, the John Birchers, the cast-offs and has-beens of the Democratic Party. . . . I just don't think a party can win nationally that way." Nevertheless the enthusiasm of the Georgia Klan became a national issue. In coastal Georgia, John Birch Society members were among the most zealous Republican workers.

Two conservative Republicans running for Congress in the Atlanta area were decisively defeated. The GOP did pick up one seat when Howard (Bo) Callaway was elected in the rural 3rd District.

Georgians read these results with quite different conclusions. GOP chairman Joseph Tribble, a staunch Goldwaterite, said: "We have just begun to fight." Any notion that the GOP must change its image "is wishful thinking on the part of the leftists." An unsuccessful candidate for the State Senate stated the moderate view succinctly: "The Republican party has to accept it—it didn't win a victory in Georgia. Every conservative, and some bigots from the Democratic party who dislike Lyndon Johnson, jumped for Goldwater, but they were not concerned with the party's overall national attitude. I hope to see a true rally of the moderates that will bring the membership of true Republicans up again. . . . I hope the Negroes can be brought back into the Republican party."

In *Alabama,* Republicans broke through to victory right down to the courthouse level. These impressive gains may well have ended the era of local Democratic endorsement of GOP presidential candidates. For Governor Wallace's tacit endorsement of the Goldwater cause has ironically left his state Democratic party totally disorganized.

As Wallace Democrats fell to Goldwater Republicans, years of amassed seniority were lost. Goldwater was opposed only by a slate of unpledged electors (President Johnson's name was not on the ballot). Straight Republican voting in some areas swept in virtually anyone the party had taken the time to nominate.

The Montgomery Advertiser described the five new Republican congressmen as political "unknowns" who were "total strangers to most Alabamians." One example of the GOP blitz came in Montgomery County where a 68 percent vote won for Republicans the probate judgeship, four places on the Board of Revenue and three places on the school board. In ten counties Republicans won every race they entered.

How permanent these gains will be is a very different question. Signs of what may be coming appeared in Macon county which elected a racially mixed Democratic slate—the first time in ninety-two years that Alabama has elected any Negroes to county office.

Mississippi was the high point of Goldwater success in 1964. In a direct showdown with President Johnson, the Republican candidate polled a stunning 87 percent of the vote—this despite Governor Paul Johnson's complaint that Goldwater was "crawfishing" on the civil rights issue. With a turnout of over 400,000, Mississippi voters set a state record—but still only one-third of the adult population voted. Who were the rest? Most of them were Negroes. To dramatize the plight of Negroes who do not have the franchise, the Mississippi Freedom Democratic Party staged a mock election. The results: Johnson 59,663; Goldwater 14.

In one congressional district, Goldwater got an astounding 92 percent of the official vote and pulled to victory former Democrat Prentiss Walker, a poultry farmer and first GOP congressman from the state in nearly 100 years. He defeated incumbent W. Arthur Winstead, a veteran of twenty-two years in the House who was in line for the chairmanship of the Armed Services subcommittee responsible for Reserve and National Guard policy. The Republican decision not to contest other seats (in order to mollify Democrats and obtain their votes for Goldwater) undoubtedly cost the GOP several other gains.

State Chairman Wirt Yerger made his plans clear after the election: "The war against liberalism, appeasement and immorality has just begun." There are indications, however, that more moderate elements in the Mississippi party might provide a counterforce to Yerger's approach.

In *Louisiana*, Goldwater's victory was not accompanied by other

Republican wins. His vote was impressive, particularly in view of the registration figures which show that only 17,474 of the state's 1,196,708 voters were Republicans. It must be remembered, however, that President Eisenhower carried the state in 1956. No seats were gained in Congress; four of the eight incumbents were not even opposed. The most important source of future Republican strength lies in the registering of Negroes, but the 1964 campaign did much to hurt the party's appeal with these voters.

The Republican defeat in *Florida* is a model in miniature of Goldwater's problems throughout the country. The state's fourteen electoral votes had been in GOP hands since 1952.

The civil rights issue brought Goldwater some votes but it cost him even more. Negro registration had increased 65 percent since 1960 and some Negro precincts went as high as fifty-to-one for Johnson. Social security and medicare were also crucial issues, as 11 percent of Florida's voters are sixty-five or over. In traditionally Republican Pinellas County, which Nixon had carried easily, Johnson won by about 20,000 votes. The small GOP delegation in the state legislature was depleted even further. The election taught some lessons. The Executive Chairman of the Republican organization in Dade County (Miami) has demanded a moderate course in the future: "After a defeat like this—you'd be kind of foolish to go down the same course again."

Goldwater had to win *Texas* to have the slightest hope of winning the presidency. It was here that his presidential boom started, here lay his greatest financial and organizational support. Here Republicans hoped to win a second Senate seat, to increase their congressional strength and to add to their state legislative triumphs. And it was here, as nowhere else, that the Goldwater experiment proved a disaster to conservative Republicans.

Goldwater received the lowest Republican vote in sixteen years. Native son Lyndon Johnson carried Texas by 63.3 percent. Perhaps more important was the surprise defeat of George Bush, oilman son of former Connecticut Senator Prescott Bush and an able and responsible conservative. Most observers had given the nod to Bush, who had the help of many of Democratic Governor John Connally's associates. But incumbent Senator Ralph W. Yarborough won a 350,000 vote victory nevertheless. This can be attributed largely to the stigma attached by minority groups to all Republicans because of Goldwater. Yarborough—the only southern senator to vote for the civil rights bill, gained 97 percent of the Negro vote (300,000) and 85 percent of the Mexican vote.

For the first time in history, the GOP ran a full slate of twenty-three Congressional candidates in the hope that they would improve on the two seats they were then holding. The bright dream turned into a nightmare. No seats were gained; the two they had were lost. And only one of Texas' seven GOP state legislators survived L.B.J.'s sweep of L.B.J.'s state.

In *Arkansas,* despite the defeat of the national ticket and of his own gubernatorial campaign, Winthrop Rockefeller has built the hard core of a permanent Republican party. It is a party similar to those constructed during the Eisenhower years in Virginia, North Carolina, and Florida—very different from the "fly by night" temporary groupings in the deep South. One evidence of this is that Nixon's Arkansas performance in 1960 was significantly better than Goldwater's in 1964.

In the Governor's race, Democrat Orval E. Faubus won once again. Newspaper reports indicate that a considerable portion of the vote was miscounted and it is probable that Rockefeller came very close to beating the veteran incumbent. Faubus used all sorts of appalling techniques to keep his vote in line. His rhetoric was typically flamboyant: "The first time they lay down in the street to block the traffic . . . they're going to get run over. And if no one else will do it, I'll get in a truck and do it myself." Rockefeller endorsed Goldwater but seldom mentioned him. With 43 percent of the total vote he doubled the previous Republican high mark. His chances for 1966 appear excellent.

GREAT LAKES STATES

The costs of the defeat in *Ohio* will be felt for some time to come. No loss was more shocking or significant than that of Robert Taft, Jr., who failed in his Senate bid by just 17,000 votes while Goldwater lost the state by more than a million. Taft had several advantages over his opponent: his strong organizational and financial support, wide newspaper backing and a name, a record, and a philosophy which appealed to Ohio. But the Goldwater issue beat him. He agreed with Goldwater in his support for a balanced budget and smaller government. But he disagreed on matters such as the test ban treaty, the UN, and civil rights. Taft wanted to keep his party solidified so that he might be reasonably effective after victory—but in so doing he risked too much identification with Goldwater. In any normal campaign, a candidate of Taft's stature would not even have to assume such a risk, much less find it to be decisive. Similarly, on the congressional scene, four seats were lost due to the weakness at the top of the ticket.

Ohio gave Richard Nixon his greatest victory in 1960. It may have dealt the Republican party its most severe loss in 1964.

In *Indiana,* the Democrats carried the presidential vote for the first time since 1936, despite strong pockets of conservatism, sharp divisions in the Democratic party, and a potential white backlash in the northern part of the state. Goldwater lost a state he had counted on—and by more than 250,000 votes. The party also lost control of the lower house of the legislature. Democrats won races for governor, senator, lieutenant governor, six state administrative positions, one seat on the state supreme court, and five seats on the appellate court. They took two congressional seats away· from the GOP.

The moderate Republican candidate for Governor lost his bid to a political novice. There were strong indications that many Goldwater Republicans voted for the Democratic candidate to avoid giving Lt. Governor Ristine control of the state party. And, as in many states, the loss of the state legislature was particularly significant since a reapportionment show-down was approaching.

Goldwater needed *Illinois* in 1964. He spent a good deal of time and money there. He lost with less than 41 percent of the vote and pulled one congressman, two potential congressmen, the state legislative ticket, and the able Charles Percy to defeat with him. Nixon had carried 93 of the 102 counties; Goldwater carried only 23.

Percy lost his bid for the Governorship because Goldwater was the candidate and Percy didn't know what to do about it. Sometimes he refused to mention Goldwater's name, and at other times (as when he introduced William Miller in San Francisco) he identified himself with the ticket. He often tried to avoid a commitment—by saying that he would vote with the majority of the convention delegation, by absenting himself during the civil rights vote at the National Convention. Percy's ambiguity on the Goldwater question was understandable, in view of the acute division in the Illinois party, but fatal—for it undermined his most positive political advantage, his reputation as a man of unbending principle. The heavy Negro vote against Goldwater hurt Percy, who had not sufficiently distinguished his own views from Goldwater's to survive.

Wisconsin gave the Johnson–Humphrey ticket 62 percent of its vote. Again the effects were felt down the line. The GOP lost two seats in Congress, the state offices of Attorney General and Lt. Governor, control of the state assembly, two seats in the state senate, and thirty-two county offices. In the senatorial contest, popular moderate Republican Wilbur Renk—like Percy and Taft and so many others—had to walk the tightrope—neither identifying with Goldwater nor repudiating him. Renk almost succeeded, running 142,000 votes ahead of the national leader. He lost by 112,000 votes to William Proxmire, who thus became the first Democrat ever elected to two full, consecutive Senate terms from the Badger State.

Two right-wing congressmen were beaten in Wisconsin. Both were strong Goldwater supporters in supposedly safe districts. In the race for Governor, Republican candidate Warren Knowles commented, "In a non-Presidential year I would swamp Reynolds." As it was he was fortunate to win—by only 19,000 votes out of the 1,700,000 cast.

In *Michigan,* it was apparent from the outset that Senator Goldwater had written off Michigan and that Governor George W. Romney had written off Goldwater. Both strategies proved sage.

There can be no doubt that Governor Romney's smashing success was due to his conspicuous disinterest in the Goldwater–Miller ticket. He collected many votes simply because he had "stood up to Goldwater." His staff predicted that he could win only if Johnson were held to a 600,000 vote plurality. As it was he outdistanced Goldwater by enough to survive a 1,075,000 vote Johnson margin. His win can be attributed in part to the economic boom and resultant increase in state revenues that blessed Romney's tenure as Governor. The minority vote was also significant. Romney increased his support in Negro wards from 12 percent in 1962 to 25 percent in 1964, while the Goldwater–Miller ticket attracted barely 2 to 3 percent of the Negro vote.

The campaign was not an easy one for the popular Governor. Chief GOP fund raiser, Arthur Summerfield, diverted substantial funds to the sole use of Goldwater forces, leaving Romney to shift for himself. In parts of the state, Goldwaterites condemned the Governor's "liberal" policies. Twenty Goldwater Gals appeared at a Romney function in Dowagiac with homemade signs reading "Goldwater yes, Romney no." The Michigan electorate reversed the slogan.

THE FARM STATES

Probably the greatest surprise of the 1964 election was the Johnson landslide in the traditionally Republican farm states. The Goldwater strategists had, since mid-1963, considered these states "safe" for the conservative Arizonan. The national Draft Goldwater movement had stressed the importance of fusing the "conservative" farm states with the South in a new winning coalition. Yet in November, 1964, the Republican parties in these areas reeled under blows as heavy as those experienced in any region of the country.

Seven of the twenty-two Republican seats in the House of Representatives fell. Democrats seized control of the state legislature in Iowa and the lower house in North Dakota. Elsewhere, they drastically increased their legislative and local office strength.

The Republican disaster in *Iowa* was unparalleled. Goldwater lost the state; the Democrats swept all state offices: five of the six Republican congressional seats were lost; the Republicans not only lost control of both houses of the state legislature but watched as Democrats won 101 of 124 lower house seats and 35 of 50 state Senate seats.

Johnson's plurality was 284,000 votes (with 61.9 percent of the total vote). He carried 93 of 99 counties. Nixon had carried 93 in 1960. Iowa Chairman Robert Ray blamed Goldwater's defeat on these factors: (1) farmers feared he would endanger price supports, (2) old people feared he would endanger social security, and (3) all people feared he would endanger peace.

The lone Republican congressional survivor, H. R. Gross, escaped with 50.1 percent of the total vote and an election challenge which was not decided until late 1965. All five lost seats can be rewon in 1966, but the youth of the Democratic officeholders and the accretion of Democratic organizational strength will force the GOP to fight hard for every one of these normally Republican seats.

Though *Kansas* has only seven electoral votes, it was considered a key element in Goldwater's campaign. Because of Kansas' strong GOP tradition, any dissatisfaction among rank and file Republicans with the Goldwater candidacy would be clearly evident. It was. Normally safe Kansas gave Goldwater only 45 percent of its vote—the same state that delivered 61 percent of its vote to Richard Nixon in 1960.

All five Kansas Republican congressional candidates held their seats. In the 1st District, Bob Dole, a staunch Goldwater backer, squeaked into his third term by less than 8,000 votes of 218,000 cast. By contrast, in the 3rd District, incumbent Robert Ellsworth, member of the Wednesday Club and a Scranton supporter, won handily.

GOP gubernatorial candidate William H. Avery, who backed Goldwater, won by the small margin of 33,000 votes, compared to the usual minimum Republican plurality of 100,000. The close vote was especially surprising because Avery, dean of the Kansas congressional delegation, was well-known, highly popular, and ran a well-financed campaign. Avery received 52 percent of the vote.

In *Nebraska,* only one notable electoral success kept Republican spirits from being crushed. Senator Roman L. Hruska's firm victory was the more impressive since Goldwater was defeated by Johnson and carried three of the other six state-wide office seekers to defeat.

The results were not a complete surprise. In the Nebraska primary earlier that year, Goldwater had received less than half the vote, despite the fact that his name was the only one on the ballot.

If there had been any doubt, the 1964 elections made a genuine two-party state out of traditionally Republican *North Dakota*. A Democratic Governor and Senator were re-elected. The Goldwater debacle cost the Republicans one of two House seats, numerous lower state-wide offices and control of the state legislature.

Moderate incumbent Republican Congressman Mark Andrews barely squeaked through in the 1st District. In the 2nd District, three-term Republican Don L. Short lost to State Senator Rolland Redlin, who tied Short to Goldwater by highlighting their joint opposition to the wheat–cotton bill, the 1961 Water Pollution Control Act, and the 1964 "anti-poverty" bill. Short, a strong Goldwater supporter, had led both tickets in the 1960 voting.

The lower house of the state legislature passed to the Democrats for the first time in history, and the defeat of the Republican national ticket also inflicted large losses in the Republican majority in the state Senate.

North Dakota's electoral vote went Democratic in 1964 for the first time since 1936. Perhaps this jolt, combined with other more immediate losses at all levels, will help to revitalize what had become an increasingly complacent state Republican organization.

Traditionally Republican *South Dakota* in 1964 supported a Democratic presidential candidate for only the third time in its entire seventy-five year history. While Nixon had won the state by 51,000, Goldwater lost it by 33,000. The feeling of uneasiness with the conservative Arizonan was summed up by one housewife: "The farmer is hurting too much to have a radical in there. . . . All he [Goldwater] has is a bunch of slams."

The two congressional seats, both Republican, were retained but with winning margins dramatically decreased from 1962. The poor Goldwater showing turned an expected romp by Lt. Governor Nils Boe, the Republican gubernatorial candidate, into a squeaker. Boe emerged with 51.7 percent of the total vote, and a margin of only 10,000. Nearly one-third of the Republican seats were lost in both the upper and lower house to imperil long-time Republican control of both.

Goldwater's 36 percent of the vote was the poorest showing of any presidential candidate in *Minnesota* since 1936. The vote was a repudiation of Goldwater more than an endorsement of Johnson. Senator Humphrey brought strength to the ticket in Minnesota; his vote for Vice President was 6.3 percent greater than his Senatorial vote in 1960. Also a factor was Republican candidate Miller's choice of Minnesota and its ultra-liberal 8th Congressional District as the setting for his charge that Humphrey was "blind on Communism."

Of Minnesota's eighty-seven counties, eighty-four went Democratic. In the agricultural south, Goldwater's farm policies frightened dozens of Republican precincts into the Democratic column for the first time in history. In the city of St. Paul, Johnson more than doubled Kennedy's winning margin. Hennepin County (including Minneapolis), won by Nixon in 1960, went two to one for Johnson.

Incumbent Democrat Eugene J. McCarthy handily won re-election to his Senate seat. His able Republican opponent, Wheelock Whitney, ran 50,000 votes ahead of Goldwater, with whom he only nominally affiliated himself.

In the races for Congress, the two out-and-out Goldwater enthusiasts sustained the worst losses. One of them, John M. Drexler, lost by 88,000 votes (carrying 27 percent) but claimed: "I was beaten by moderate Republicans—Benedict Arnolds—who sponsored a write-in candidate who got only 322 votes, but hurt my cause seriously." The four incumbent Republican congressmen all won re-election by distinguishing themselves from Goldwater.

The big story of the 1964 election in Minnesota is that a strong "moderate" state Republican organization, under the expert leadership of Robert Forsythe, hung on as well as it did in the face of the anti-Goldwater blitz.

THE WEST: THE ROCKY MOUNTAIN STATES

The band of states that span the mountain ranges between the Great Plains and the Pacific coastal states was the heart of Goldwater country. The Senator from Arizona counted on his people for even more solid support than they had given Richard Nixon in 1960. Their rejection (all but Arizona) must have been one of the cruelest aspects of defeat.

Montana went Democratic for the first time since 1948. Johnson's margin (59 percent) was exceeded by Democratic Senator Mike Mansfield (64 percent). The combination produced a purge of Montana's Republican officeholders. Conservative Republican Governor Tim Babcock needed extraordinary split-ticket voting to retain his office. Only his incumbency saved him in a Democratic campaign against "Babcock, Birchism, and backwater" that singled out Babcock's refusal to proclaim United Nations day.

Idaho was one of Goldwater's near misses (49.1 percent). The strong party leadership of Republican Governor Robert E. Smylie accounted for some gains in the state legislature, but was unable to pull Barry Goldwater into the "win" column. In one of the few Republican congressional advances outside of the South, George V. Hansen upset two-term Democratic incumbent Ralph R. Harding. Harding apparently pushed the extremism issue too hard with a personal attack on Ezra Taft Benson, a leader in the Mormon

Church, for supporting the John Birch Society. Hansen benefited from the religious resentment that resulted.

Utah offered Republicans the prospect of a new Senate seat. With Goldwater at the head of the ticket, they instead lost a Governorship, a congressional seat, and control of both houses of the state legislature. Democrat Frank E. Moss rode to the Senate in 1958 only by the grace of J. Bracken Lee's conservative third party, and was considered even by the Democratic National Committee to be a certain casualty in 1964. But he was blessed by the nomination of Goldwater, by a bitter moderate–conservative Republican primary fight that left unhealed scars, and by the fact that the conservative Goldwater supporter, Ernest L. Wilkinson, won that Republican primary.

The trend in *Wyoming* was similar. Again, Republicans failed to win a Senate seat they had lost in 1958 and expected to regain. Republican John S. Wold, State Chairman since 1960, failed to oust Democratic incumbent Senator Gale McGee. President Johnson's appearance as a conservative, not an "ultra," probably helped gloss over McGee's own record which was considerably more liberal.

Right to work was probably important in Goldwater's loss of Wyoming; it was a controversial position easily attached to him. A major union effort was mounted with the result that the Republican share of the labor vote dropped from an estimated 50 percent in 1962 to less than 25 percent in 1964. Republicans also lost the state's single congressional seat and control of the lower house of the state legislature.

Colorado went Democratic in a presidential election for the first time in sixteen years. In 1964, Republican candidates lost every race for a major political office in the state. No charge can be made that Goldwater lacked support from local Republican officials. Governor John Love, a preconvention supporter of Governor Scranton, campaigned hard for Goldwater–Miller both inside and outside the state. When asked how long after the nomination he had decided to support the Arizona conservative, Love replied, "About three seconds."

Republicans lost both their congressmen—Donald G. Brotzman and J. Edgar Chenoweth, although *The Denver Post* had given Chenoweth better than a fifty-to-forty lead in the polls, Republicans lost 45 percent of their seats and control of the lower house.

Another near miss for the Senate came in *Nevada,* which Goldwater lost by a margin approximately ten times as great as Nixon's deficit in 1960. Howard Cannon was one of the most vulnerable Democratic senators, elected with the oversized Democratic class of 1958. His opponent, Republican Lt. Governor Paul Laxalt, waged a vigorous, conservative campaign (he admitted he would have voted against the civil rights bill). Cannon tied Laxalt to Goldwater and refused to debate him: "I am not sure my opponent would know the issues . . . unless he studied very hard." Cannon won the race by a razor thin margin that was contested unsuccessfully by the Republicans.

Even Goldwater's win in *Arizona* was a disappointment. The Arizona Senator barely carried his home state, with 50.5 percent of the vote! Goldwater's difficulties here reflected many of his problems nationally. The editorial in *The Arizona Daily Star* was merely a hometown version of a national reaction:

> Old friends have a right to differ when it comes to policies involving the very fate, not only of our nation, but of civilization itself. Arizona should be proud of the accomplishments of Barry Goldwater, but that should not mean that when he champions such a reckless foreign policy, they should vote for him for President.

Also familiar were the words of the Phoenix NAACP President: "Mr. Goldwater says we have no problems, but indeed Phoenix parades under a banner of conservatism which is a coverup for a system of denials and discrimination and which makes the rich richer and the poor poorer."

In key state-wide races, retiring Governor Paul J. Fannin, Arizona's best Republican vote-getter in history, needed considerable help from his opponent to win a Senate seat. Democrat Roy L. Elson suffered from Lyndon Johnson's receipt of an endorsement by California Governor Pat Brown, anathema in Arizona, which desperately needs California's water.

Goldwater aide Richard Kleindienst lost the Republican State House to a Democrat whom Fannin had beaten handily two years earlier. Kleindienst suffered from a rugged primary and from adverse reaction to his aggressive personality. His sharp losses in Mexican–American wards clinched his defeat.

Goldwater's presence on the ballot did little to help Arizona Republican candidates. They ran, as usual, as individuals without much reference to the party organization.

The last of the states in this grouping, *New Mexico,* followed the regional trend. Goldwater imposed a 60,000 vote deficit on New Mexico Republicans by obtaining 40 percent of the popular vote. This cost the New Mexico GOP one congressional seat and may have been instrumental in the loss of a Republican seat in the U.S. Senate. Incumbent Republican Edwin L. Mechem allied himself firmly with Goldwater: "We are against the junk that's coming out of Washington today." His opponent, Congressman Joseph Montoya, consistently advertised Mechem's support of the Republican candidate by calling him "a shadow of Senator Goldwater." Most observers thought that this marginal race would be decided by the presidential race. It apparently was.

Here, as elsewhere, the 1964 returns showed that the Goldwater candidacy hurt the conservative Republicans even more than it damaged the moderates.

THE WEST: THE PACIFIC STATES

Republicans had counted heavily on gains in the far west—with some of the fastest growing population centers in the country. This was the dynamic, restless America that the Goldwater strategists had hoped to tap. Everywhere they were disappointed.

Washington, whose voters have a tradition of split-ticket voting, set the pattern. A Nixon plurality of some 30,000 in 1960 disappeared in a 300,000 Goldwater deficit. Yet an attractive thirty-nine year old Republican, Daniel J. Evans, ousted two-term Democrat Albert D. Rosellini from the Governorship by about 148,000 votes. Evans, a former Seattle engineer and leader of the state House Republicans, has since received national attention as the nation's youngest governor and as a potential Republican star. Evans' fine political organization and personal appeal were the key to his victory. The Goldwater State Chairman was a respected and hard-working organizer but his product just did not sell.

Popular Democratic Senator Henry "Scoop" Jackson easily defeated his Republican opponent, who had strongly endorsed Goldwater, with about 72 percent of the vote. The biggest surprise came in the congressional races where incumbent GOP Congressmen Jack Westland, Walt Horan, Bill Stinson, and Thor Tollefson were all defeated by Democratic newcomers. Three of the losses were clear upsets, attributable to Goldwater, a slate of aggressive and attractive Democratic candidates, and the active intervention of Senator Jackson. In the state House of Representatives, Republicans also lost heavily.

Oregon followed suit. Lukewarm Hatfield support for Goldwater could not prevent a stunning reversal from 1960. Yet Tom McCall, the Republican candidate for Secretary of State, the top state constitutional office up for grabs in 1964, won by running over 140,000 votes ahead of the national ticket. McCall had refused to support Senator Goldwater and as a consequence his access to normal supplies of campaign funds had been severed. Incumbent Republican Treasurer Belton was narrowly defeated (51.4 percent) in an upset apparently aided by the Goldwater undertow. Republicans made limited gains in the state legislature, winning control of the lower house for the first time in several years.

The biggest prize of them all, *California,* had been the capstone of the Goldwater nomination drive. In early calculations of electoral votes, the Senator's strategists had listed California as "doubtful." California voters indeed had doubts. They gave Lyndon B. Johnson (a would-be westerner) a plurality of some 1.3 million votes. Goldwater received his strongest support in the two centers of conservatism—Orange (55.8 percent) and San Diego (50.13 percent) counties. Northern California went heavily Democratic with normally Republican Marin County to the north of San Francisco giving the Republican ticket only 38.6 percent of its vote (a 25 percent Republican defection).

In the California Senate race, the carpetbagger issue continued to hurt Pierre Salinger. Bobby Kennedy's entry into the New York race and the prospect of a clan of Kennedyites in the Senate only increased the public reaction. Salinger was also hurt by his strong principled opposition to Proposition 14 on the ballot (making fair housing legislation unconstitutional but phrased in terms of freedom to sell to whomever you wish). George Murphy executed a tactically outstanding campaign while moving from conservative to moderate positions on several issues. Although he endorsed Goldwater, he specifically broke with him on the civil rights bill and the test ban treaty. His win was clearly a personal triumph.

In congressional races and the state legislature, Republicans generally held their own or made slight gains. The party had been building since 1958 when William Knowland and the right to work forces brought it to total defeat. In 1964, Goldwater, the Knowland choice, deprived California Republicans of substantial gains.

Commenting on the election, one California Republican leader wryly noted: "You made the choice, now listen to that echo."

To the north, *Alaska* went to Johnson by a slightly larger percentage margin than Washington and Oregon. Republican House candidate Lowell Thomas, Jr. narrowly missed upsetting incumbent Democrat Ralph J. Rivers. Republicans lost seats in both houses of the state legislature. Again, a Republican party that had been building steadily was dealt a stunning setback that will be hard to overcome soon.

Hawaii completes our summary of state races. The racially mixed islands gave Goldwater one of his smallest totals—about 22 percent! But Republican Senator Hiram L. Fong was re-elected, in another startling example of split-ticket voting, by a 52.9 percent vote. Fong steered clear of Goldwater and got a big assist from the powerful Hawaiian International Longshore Workers Union.

The Goldwater candidacy cost the Hawaiian Republican party nothing. But it prevented the probable election of a new Republican congressman and substantial gains in both houses of the State Legislature. More importantly, in the formative years of the Islanders' voting development, the Goldwater candidacy may have made many a Democratic inclination into a habit and this in a state that achieved its statehood under a Republican administration.

And so it went across the nation. Republicans everywhere were struck by the magnitude of the disaster. In shock and disbelief they asked themselves how this could have happened. What could be done, now, to save the Republican party?

Part Two

"The Elephant on the Brink: Where Do We Go from Here?"

There was an element of inevitability in the Goldwater disaster. Some of the Senator's staunchest supporters who were running for election saw it coming and fled from the national ticket. Republican moderates retreated to defend their states and districts until the delusion had run its course and the American voters had spent their fury on the Goldwater Republican party.

But what would moderates do when the election was over? Could they again take control of their party? Could they reshape it and alter its image? Their early attempts are chronicled and evaluated in Chapter 4.

Chapter 5 presents the heart of the message that the men and women of Ripon would like to share with the Republican party. That message is that we stand on the brink of a new and exciting political era. Our discussion attempts to outline the general shape of that era. Chapter 6 goes on to ask young Americans to plunge themselves into its concerns. It presents once again—to use the words that have become the motto of the Ripon Society—"A Call to Excellence in Leadership."

4

THE REPUBLICAN RESPONSE
TO DEFEAT

FOR MANY observers, the results of the 1964 election were never in doubt. Their real question was, "How will the Republican party respond to defeat?" Would it re-emerge as a strong second party or would it linger for a while—a dying, crippled minority party, unable to re-establish direction and momentum, waiting helplessly for the opposition to engulf it?

This question was not answered in the weeks and months that followed the election. It has not been answered yet. But those who looked carefully at the Republican party could find much evidence for a pessimistic conclusion. For at least two important lessons can be drawn from the Republican experience in 1964 and 1965. These became evident well before November, 1964, although until then few realized their full significance.

The first conclusion was that a critical vacuum had developed in party leadership. The second was the fact that—whatever the November results—the Goldwater nomination significantly strengthened the position of the conservative movement within the Republican organization.

The Republican Leadership Vacuum

The election campaign of 1964 was, first of all, a test of Republican leadership. The assassination of President Kennedy left Lyndon B. Johnson in charge of the fortunes of the Democratic party. A progressive Republican ticket, headed by a candidate from a populous northern state, stood an excellent chance of combining normal Republican strength with some of the Independent and Democratic support Kennedy had enjoyed. It could have meant an important Republican breakthrough. At a minimum it should have resulted in continued gains in Congress and more Republican Governors. Yet the strangely effective arithmetic of the Goldwater southern strategists carried the day. When the time came to speak, no one came forth to answer on behalf of the Republican majority.

The 1964 campaign showed, once and for all, that leadership of the Republican party had passed away from the figures of the Eisenhower era. Many Americans looked to General Eisenhower, until the final hour, to stop the Goldwater nomination; but the San Francisco Convention revealed to the nation that Republican leaders of the 1950s and before—Henry Cabot Lodge, Christian Herter, Thomas E. Dewey, Herbert Brownell, Walter Kohler, Joseph Martin, Harold Stassen, Arthur B. Langlie, and the two Eisenhowers—had yielded their power. They had lost command of the party. Now, when the party needed them the most, they could not go back; they could not again pick up the reins of leadership.

So, 1964 revealed the emergence of a new leadership cadre in the Republican party—the militant young "conservatives" of the Goldwater movement, men like New York's F. Clifton White, Arizona's Dean Burch, and Alabama's John Grenier, all of whom engineered the successful drive for the nomination. San Francisco was their moment of supreme triumph, their capture of a national party in a presidential election year.

The militant young conservatives moved into a leadership vacuum which need not have existed. Several groups could have provided the Republican party with leadership during the national and party crises of late 1963 and 1964. But none did!

First, there were the Republican Governors, the most important potential base of "moderate" Republican strength in the party, the natural heirs of the Eisenhower years—Rockefeller, Scranton, Romney, Hatfield, and others.

The Republican Governors' Association had been formed at Miami in July of 1963. GOP leaders had worked together effectively at the National Governors Conference and they unanimously decided to continue this useful relationship through a formal association. Idaho Governor Robert E. Smylie, first chairman of the group, predicted that the association would emerge as a "third major force" in the party.

This dream was frustrated. The Goldwater organization foresaw the implications of a "third force" when no other Republican leadership existed. Quickly they moved to stop it. Republican National Chairman William E. Miller severed the growing liaison between Republicans in Congress and the Governors. He and his staff also prepared "articles of association" whereby the Governors were controlled by the National Committee office. The Association never did develop its own resources and was unable to act effectively as the party slipped toward disaster.*

* See "The Republican Governors' Association: The Case for a Third Force," A Ripon Society Report, December, 1964. Information on securing copies may be obtained by writing The Ripon Society, Box 138, Cambridge 38, Mass.

Nor did individual Governors emerge as leaders. Romney and Scranton were not equipped or inclined to assume national leadership until it was too late. Rockefeller's personal life unfortunately disqualified him in the eyes of too many voters. Even then, moderates looked to his California campaign as their *one and only* line of defense against the Goldwater candidacy. When he narrowly lost, it was all over.

There were other potentially effective groupings of moderate leadership: men like Thomas Kuchel, Clifford Case, Hugh Scott, and Jacob Javits in the Senate and the Wednesday Group Republicans in the House. But neither group functioned. For one thing, progressive Republican strength was diverted to combatting the long civil rights filibuster in the Senate—a Pyrrhic victory, in the final analysis, when the party chose a nominee who voted against the bill and campaigned on a platform that ignored the Republican legislative contribution. And in the House, for all the protestations of willing help, Nelson Rockefeller could find only three Republicans who were willing to read his speeches into *The Congressional Record*—a figure that William Scranton at the eleventh hour could not better.

Another possible rallying point was the Republican Citizens Committee, a nonparty organization that had been established in July, 1962, to do some of the work that the Republican National Committee was unable or unwilling to handle. As the National Committee became more openly pro-Goldwater, under Chairman Miller, the case for independent initiative from the Citizens Committee became more imperative. Senator Goldwater realized the potential and wrote a sharp letter to National Chairman Miller attacking the propriety of "irregular" extra-party organizations. He ignored the fact that former President Eisenhower was the Citizens' honorary chairman.* But whatever its potential, the Citizens Committee refused to make any choice. It remained all things to all Republicans. It managed to produce a series of position papers under Dr. Milton Eisenhower's Critical Issues Council and a useful manual, "Citizens for X," but it had no answers for the leadership problems of the Republican party.

The inability of Republican moderates to fill the developing leadership vacuum was not a good omen for the GOP future. The pre-November performance gave little indication that moderates

---

* More recently, Goldwater has also attacked the Republican Governors' Association in the same vein—as a divisive "splinter group." But he has had no qualms whatsoever about assuming the honorary chairmanship of the Free Society Association—a much more ambitious and less "regular" political and educational group.

could displace defeated Goldwaterites in the weeks and months that followed the election.

One other sizable grouping in the party could have assumed leadership in the face of the Goldwater challenge. These were the organization Republicans, the so-called "professionals" who had run the state and national campaigns in 1960 and 1962. Their ranks included seasoned veterans like Ray Bliss, Thruston Morton, and Richard Nixon. Also included were scores of state and local leaders —dedicated to their party and caring above all that it should win.

They were the "career" men and women, the "political brokers" of the GOP. They were not particularly concerned with ideology. Most of them could work as diligently and as sincerely for Barry Goldwater as for Nelson Rockefeller. They were ready to do battle for John Tower and for Jacob Javits. They could look with family pride on both Strom Thurmond and Edward Brooke. "As long as they are Republicans, that's the main thing," they would say again and again.

Richard Nixon did not believe he could actively seek to fill the leadership vacuum for a number of reasons—his defeat in California, his recent move to New York, his lack of a political and financial base. As for the other "pros," they did not care to do violent battle with militant conservatives. It was not their manner of operation. They viewed themselves as healers. Now they sought to bridge a gulf that had plagued the party at least since 1912. But what most of the organization Republicans did not realize— what few of them were able to see—was that 1964 was different.

The pros made two basic miscalculations. First, they underestimated the potency of the Goldwater movement in the precincts. These "new" conservatives were a far, far different breed from the older Taft and Hoover Republicans. They played for keeps as they took over one state delegation after another. They represented something new in American politics—an ideological ferment which the organization leaders could not control.

A second miscalculation only compounded the results of the first. The professionals waited *too long* before moving to redress the imbalance between the party's two wings. Challenged from the right, they shifted support very gradually to the left and waited for equilibrium to be established. But this time they waited in vain. Rockefeller, with precious little help from outside his own organization, narrowly lost the battle they were all depending on him to win. By the time Scranton sallied forth from Harrisburg, the professionals had already begun to make their peace with the new conquerors. Some had muttered briefly, but most had gone along. The right wing was dominant; the professionals could no longer play one faction against another. Now they could only volunteer their "expertise." They could follow—and they could serve. But as brokers—and as leaders—they were unemployed. When the Cow Palace was almost empty, when the jubilant crowds that had cheered the ill-considered acceptance speech had all but left the hall, a lonely man sat amid the clutter of discarded placards and strewn paper, his head in his hands. He spoke to a friend: "For the first time I've lost all my influence with my delegation. What have we done? Bob Taft can't win now." That man, unnoticed by passers-by, was the state chairman of the Republican Party in Ohio, Mr. Ray C. Bliss.

The Hidden Costs of the Goldwater Nomination

The first conclusion about the post-November state of the Republican party, then, was that there were *no* clear successors to the leadership of the party. November, 1964, could not and would not, by itself, resolve the issue of leadership. Yet this point escaped too many Republicans who expected an automatic return to "normalcy." The second conclusion was less obvious, though potentially of far greater consequence. The very *fact* of a Goldwater nomination produced long term changes in the Republican party, most of which strengthened the hand of the "conservatives" for the post-November leadership struggle.

For months before San Francisco, Goldwater supporters had won converts with the argument that a "conservative" deserved the nomination. The slogan "a choice, not an echo" suggested the need for a *new* campaign tactic, which pointedly ignored Richard Nixon's near miss in 1960. Even liberal pundit Walter Lippmann was telling the nation in 1962 that it was safe to let the "conservatives" run Goldwater in 1964. He didn't stand a chance against the popular Kennedy and a resounding defeat would rid the Republican party of its right-wing virus once and for all. Some Republicans protested this line of thinking in 1964, but the logic of political amateurs, echoed by the Democratic left, persuaded many who should have known better. Even after San Francisco, Republicans who had opposed Goldwater waited impatiently for the end of the campaign, ignorant of how disadvantaged it would leave them. The Goldwater people regarded 1964 not as an end, but as a beginning.

In the chaotic world of American politics, the quadrennial presidential campaign is one of the few centralizing forces. For a few months the wealth and energy and talent of amateurs are joined to those of professionals, and new vitality pours into our national parties. Massive organizations recruit new workers and new dollars. The resources of the national party organization are replenished. Personalities and ideas are exposed to the bright glare of public attention. The basic direction of our government is set for the next four years.

For the Republican party in 1964, already a decided minority, the new resources of a vigorous, broad-based campaign were essential. But the nomination of Barry Goldwater set into motion quite a different sequence of events. True, an unprecedented sum of campaign funds was raised—much of it in the form of small contributions from the rank and file of the Goldwater movement. True also, a new level of campaign activity and door-bell ringing was reached—again, in good part, by the Goldwater zealots. But these impressive accomplishments were outweighed by even greater losses.

With every speech that Barry Goldwater and William Miller made, the party lost votes, and not just for this one election. To young voters, casting their presidential ballots for the first time, Goldwater–Miller were *the* symbol of the Republican party. Everywhere but in the deep South, the reverse tide was felt: in sharp declines in Republican registrations, in candidates who read the handwriting on the wall and decided not to run, in traditional Republican financial sources that began to dry up. In November came the rip-tide. Millions of Republicans left their party, and hundreds of Republican candidates—some of the finest in recent years—were pulled down by the Goldwater undertow.

The Michigan Survey Research Center estimated that young people, ages twenty-one to thirty-nine, who will constitute the center of gravity of the American electorate by the early 1970s, voted 71 percent Johson—29 percent Goldwater, the highest Democratic vote in any age group!

But this is not the whole story. For there is an element of ir-reversibility in all of these precedents. They have an inertia, a momentum of their own. *The burden of reversing them will now rest on the Republican party.* Why should a voter reregister as a Republican? Having voted for a Democrat once, why shouldn't he vote for one again? Why should the Negroes support the Republican party? Why should young people cast their lot with the GOP? Polls taken in the summer of 1965 show that Lyndon Johnson had further *consolidated* the support of Republicans who voted for him. It is idle to predict sweeping Republican gains in the congressional elections of 1966, until the Republican party tries to reclaim the Republicans who bolted in 1964! But the politics of wishful thinking is the new Republican order of the day.

One section of the Republican party, however, *did* register significant gains in the 1964 elections—the Goldwater faction. The elections greatly strengthened the young Republican parties in the states of the deep South. Seven new Republican congressmen from

Alabama, Mississippi, and Georgia added a new ultraconservative element to the depleted ranks of House Republicans. The "conversion" of Democrats such as South Carolina's Senator Strom Thurmond and Congressman Albert Watson brought even more southern "conservatives" to Republican Congressional ranks. This triggered rumors of several potential turncoats. Moreover the November results will mean increased voting strength for southern Republicans in the Republican National Committee, the Young Republican National Convention, and ultimately the National Convention of 1968. Republican states that suffered most from the Goldwater campaign—including the populous states of New York and Pennsylvania—lost representation according to party rules. Thus, ironically, those elements which had championed the southern strategy—so disastrous for the national party—were rewarded most in the coin of party influence. Those who had opposed it—who saw the implications of the strategy most clearly—were repaid for their foresight with even less power in party affairs.

The Goldwater faction also gained a financial and organizational base from which to build its intraparty position. For the first time in decades Republican moderates and liberals have lost the organizing focus of the presidential nomination. It is a hidden cost of enormous significance. A year after the campaign, the moderates have still not found a suitable focus for organization. The control of the national party apparatus conferred important benefits: organizational intelligence, party files, lists of contributors, professional staff. In the final weeks of the campaign, the Goldwater fund-drive and curtailed campaign activities yielded a sizable national surplus which remained with Goldwater-controlled committees such as the Goldwater–Miller TV Committee. The Goldwater faction had firm control of the defeated Republican party on November 4. The initiative and the energy to displace them would have to be mounted from outside.

The Months of Decision:
November, 1964–January, 1965

Those Republicans who wanted to reshape, rebuild, and redirect the Republican party after the Goldwater debacle had two initial handicaps as we have seen: a record of their own past failures in leadership and a greatly strengthened Goldwaterite cadre. This was the irony of 1964: The very actions that were destroying the Republican party as a competitor in the American two-party system were also reinforcing right-wing control of the party. As long as the leadership vacuum persisted, the Goldwater group would continue to exert disproportionate influence on party policy and strategy. The right wing was not large in absolute numbers—but as the party got smaller and smaller, their percentage of the total got bigger and bigger.

This was the true dilemma of the Republican party in November, 1964. Yet the record of non-Goldwater leaders in the crucial months that followed shows that few, even then, realized the seriousness of the Republican position and those who did had difficulty in doing anything to correct it. This *may* indicate that the suicidal trend to the right has passed beyond the point where it can be reversed. That possibility must remain the unwritten chapter of this book.

On November 4, before the election returns had been fully tabulated, the battle was clearly joined between the Goldwater high command and the moderate wing of the Republican party. The cries for new Republican leadership and a return to the political center grew into a clamor of surprising proportions. The moderates and liberals in the Republican party suddenly had a chance to gain some leverage in party councils by reminding their colleagues of the verdict which grass roots Republicans and Independents had rendered on November 3.

Both the Goldwaterites and Republican moderates had begun to develop their strategies well before the election. San Francisco had convinced many moderates, such as the younger Republicans who staffed the Rockefeller, Scranton, Lodge, and Romney teams, or who served as alternate delegates, that the fight to regain control of the party would be bitter and long. Out of defeat had come the beginnings of a new Republican leadership group. Hardly noticed in the shadow of moderate Republican generals or the young Goldwater lieutenants, these men and women began meeting and working with new determination before the San Francisco Convention adjourned.

By November, several plans of action had been developed and circulated among moderate Republican leaders. The most detailed of those programs called for moderates to make a frontal assault for control at all levels of the national party: the Republican National Committee, the Republican leadership in Congress, the Senatorial and Congressional Campaign Committees, the Republican Governors' Association, the Republican State Chairmen's Association, etc. The "frontal strategy" was based on the assumption that Republican moderates had a limited time in which to work. The deadline, it was assumed, would come in January. The election had shocked many Republicans into a state of political realism. They were ready to do *something* to get the Republican party back into the political center. But this spirit would be dissipated when Congress reconvened and public attention shifted to the Johnson legislative program. There was no time to waste.

The Goldwater strategists had also been developing plans. Their first and admitted objective had been control of the Republican party, not the presidency. They were not about to accept any election verdict as a mandate for them to step down from the positions they had gained at great effort and cost. Preserve as much as possible, this was the key to the post-election strategy. The Republican moderates would have to dislodge them from positions of power one by one. Here too, time was critical. Temporarily disadvantaged, the "conservative" cadre had to fight for time—time to let passions and memories simmer and cool, time to let amateurs and volunteers among the moderates drift back to detachment and noninvolvement, time to re-establish a sense of politics as usual. Then the conservatives could wield their most useful weapons— dedicated energy and effective organization—with maximum effect.

The immediate strategy of the conservative right was to distract the moderate attack—a strategy that, in retrospect, worked all too well. National Chairman Dean Burch provided a convenient target to draw opposition fire. If the test over his leadership were lost, the right would lose one of its own at the Republican National Committee. But perhaps conservatives could still wield influence in the selection of Burch's successor. And meanwhile, no one would be paying attention to maneuvers on the congressional front, where the real power stakes lay. If, by chance, the moderates lost the fight to replace Burch, this would be a tremendous symbolic victory for the "conservative cause." But in either case, the conservative high command did not swallow the myth which most moderates accepted—that a change in the National Chairman, *by itself,* represented a significant change in the direction of the Republican party.

Precious days slipped away as moderate Republican leaders dispersed for their first real vacation since before San Francisco. The Republican Governors met in December. The Republican National Committee was called into session in late January. It was soon clear that the moderates had adopted a *limited* strategy; they were simply out to replace Burch! Implicitly, the frontal strategy had been rejected. The moderate chieftains and their divided supporters were not moving toward a disciplined or aggressive alliance.

Although they had been vindicated by the election results, they did not even attempt to construct a strong counter-organization to take the party home again. The leadership vacuum did not disappear, though several leaders wrote a few bold words into generally cautious statements. They entered the largely symbolic contest for the National Chairmanship but did little else.

The key to the moderates' limited strategy was the selection of Ohio's chairman, Ray C. Bliss, as their replacement for Dean Burch. The Republican Governors, resolved to strengthen their voice in the party, had unanimously taken a strong anti-Burch position in Denver, though they did not mention Burch's name. Moderate strategists such as George Hinman of the Rockefeller organization and Craig Truax, Scranton's Pennsylvania state chairman, moved behind the scenes through National Committeemen like Ross of Nebraska to engineer the transfer. It was thought essential that the move to replace Burch look as much as possible like a move of Midwesterners against right-wingers and as little as possible like a moderate takeover. The epithet "Eastern Liberal Establishment" was still too potent to permit any open moderate involvement. The limited strategy led to the selection of a traditional party professional as the moderates' candidate.

Thus at the point of time when they had, in relative terms, their maximum resources, the moderates chose the cautious approach— seeking broad support for a popular compromise candidate. They avoided a direct confrontation with the Goldwater faction on any other issue.

It was not intended that Ray Bliss would lead a moderate renaissance but moderates hoped that he would not discourage it. As a first step, moderates could argue that the limited strategy made sense.

The problem was that too few moderates realized that this was *only* a first step. The selection of Bliss—as he himself emphasized— meant that the moderates would *not* take control of the party. The Bliss election was a defeat for the right wing, but—*in and of itself* —it was not a victory for the moderates.

The Republican National Committee convened in a cold, rainy Chicago for a three-day January meeting. Bliss was named chairman without the excitement of formal battle, but in the tense, emotion-charged atmosphere that accompanies a transfer of power. Control passed from the Goldwater right back to the party professionals. Once again they had assumed power as the political brokers of Republican politics. As the Republican party drifted without direction they sought to re-establish a balance between the two Republican factions.

The National Committee fight was a battle over an important symbol. But Republican moderates faced three other important opportunities between November and January. With their attention diverted to the National Committee fight, however, little was done to encourage a coordinated moderate Republican effort elsewhere. As a result, the moderates lost openings that would be hard to regain.

The first area of moderate action concerned Republican citizens organizations. Two weeks after the election, representatives of several Republican groups met in New York to coordinate their activities. Included were such organizations as the Committee to Support Moderate Republicans chaired by Charles P. Taft, former Republican Mayor of Cincinnati (later reconstituted in Washington, D.C., as Republicans For Progress under Executive Director Albert E. Abrahams); The National Negro Republican Assembly which formed after the San Francisco Convention; the National Conference of Republican Workshops; the new Committee of '68 headed by Warren J. Sinsheimer, former national chairman of the "Draft Scranton" movement; and the Ripon Society. Other prominent Republican citizens such as former Governor Elmer L. Andersen of Minnesota, who became the chairman of the steering committee that emerged from the meeting, also joined in the discussion.

Again the moderates could not agree on a frontal strategy. Many wished to defer such questions to the top echelon of moderate leadership. The existence of the Republican Citizens Committee was used as an argument against the formation of a new large-scale citizens organization. The group decided to send representatives to the December meeting of the Republican Governors in Denver and to meet again in full session *after* the issue of the national chairmanship had been resolved.

Out of that meeting grew the Council of Republican Organizations—a possible new rallying point for moderate forces. The group has received considerable attention with statements on important national issues. But by the time of the second meeting of the Council in early February, much of the public sympathy and emotional support that might have been tapped by a resurgent Republican citizens movement in November or December was gone.

The second area of moderate Republican initiative was the Republican Governors' Association. The Governors' meeting in December, 1964, at Denver was the moderate Republican summit. Most of the Republican Governors were in attendance. Republican Congressmen Ogden Reid of New York and Alphonzo Bell of California sat as representatives of the moderate "Wednesday Group" of House Republicans. Representatives of the nascent Council of Republican Organizations were also present. Aides to the Governors and various national committeemen held concurrent meetings.

The Ripon Society had helped to set the tone of the Denver

meeting by the release of a Ripon Society report, "The Republican Governors' Association: The Case for a Third Force," just prior to the December meeting. The Ripon report called on the Governors to establish themselves as a leadership force, with staff and independent financing, within the Republican party. The report traced the history of the Republican Governors' Association and analyzed some of the reasons for its ineffectiveness in the pre-San Francisco period.

In addition to endorsing the strategy to replace Chairman Burch, the Governors resolved to hire a permanent staff and open headquarters in Washington. They agreed to independent financing and the establishment of a program and policy committee and gubernatorial campaign committee. The Governors' Association thus laid the basis for becoming a dynamic and constructive force within the Republican party.

But again, the thrust was blunted. Governor Robert E. Smylie, Chairman of the Association, arrived in Chicago in January prepared to announce the opening of the Governors' headquarters. The announcement was never made. Months later, negotiations on this matter between the new National Chairman and the Governors were still in progress. An important moderate initiative had been temporarily lost. The Governors did open their office on September 1, 1965, and reawakened hopes that they would be able to focus public attention on progressive and constructive Republicans.

The poorest performance by Republican moderates came in the third area of activity, the congressional Republican party. One initiative for revamping party operations in Congress came not from the moderates but from Missouri Republican Thomas B. Curtis, a constructive conservative in the Taft tradition. In mid-November, Curtis asked for an extraordinary session of the House Republican Conference in December. He called for a basic change in the "techniques of leadership" and suggested several specific improvements.

Curtis got the meeting he asked for, but not the program. The special December meeting of the House Republican Conference did, however, provide an opportunity to reassess the leadership of Minority Leader Charles Halleck of Indiana. He was marked for replacement. Given the conservative weighting of House Republicans—many from safe districts that had survived even the worst of the Roosevelt landslides in the 1930s—it was quite clear that Republican moderates could not elect one of their own to the leadership. But they could hold the balance of power in a fluid situation. Potential successors to Halleck included Congressman Gerald Ford of Michigan, who had been elected Conference Chairman by a Young Turk insurrection two years earlier, and conservative Congressman Melvin Laird of Wisconsin.

Laird had been Chairman of the 1964 platform committee. In 1960, he had been passed over for that job and given the Vice Chairmanship because he was considered "too conservative." But in 1964, he had clearly dominated the writing of the platform. He had the votes to support him on every issue. When Congressman Silvio Conte of Massachusetts challenged the procedures Laird was using in hearings and drafting sessions, Laird's reply was a threat to release the Wisconsin delegation—then pledged to favorite-son Congressman John Byrnes—to Goldwater.

In the wake of the rough treatment that moderates had received in San Francisco, their relationships with Laird were anything but cordial.

Shortly after the Conference met, a small group began to plan Halleck's overthrow. They soon decided to coalesce behind Ford rather than Laird, who was too controversial. When Ford vacated the Conference Chairmanship to run for leader, it was assumed that Laird would make a bid for that post.

Two alternative strategies were open to moderates in the House. They could cast a bloc vote for Ford or Halleck, striking the best bargain they could for subsidiary posts such as the Chairmanship of the Congressional Campaign Committee. Or they could, as a group, stay neutral on the fight for Minority Leader and concentrate their full energies on challenging Laird for the Conference chairmanship. In either case, the "Wednesday Group" would provide the shock troops.

When the smoke of battle had cleared, the moderates had nothing! On the Ford–Halleck contest the early desertion of two key members to Ford had weakened the credibility of the bloc vote strategy. The Ford lieutenants decided they didn't need any agreements with the moderate forces. An apparent last-minute shift to Halleck came too late if it was a serious strategy. As for Conference chairmanship, the "Wednesday Group" fielded a last-minute candidate, Congressman Peter Frelinghuysen of New Jersey. His near miss only underlined how ineffectively the moderates were using the leverage they had. The final blow came when Frelinghuysen, Ford's choice for minority whip, was defeated by incumbent Leslie Arends of Illinois in a stunning reversal for the new leader. So demoralized were the moderates that there was not even token opposition to the election of John Rhodes of Arizona, a top Goldwater leader in the House, to the chairmanship of the House Republican Policy Committee.

In the Senate things were no better for moderate Republicans. Most of the discontent actually came from associates of the defeated Senator from Arizona. Efforts were made to purge the Republican whip, Senator Thomas Kuchel of California, on the charge that he had not campaigned for the Goldwater–Miller ticket. The moderates on the other hand, did not seek to unseat Iowa's conservative Senator Bourke Hickenlooper, Chairman of the Republican Policy Committee in the Senate. Nor did they challenge any other leaders. When the Senate convened it was clear that there would be no fight from the moderates. In return, Tom Kuchel could keep the whip post.

Such was the moderate Republican response to defeat. Added to the handicaps the party had inherited from the 1964 campaign was a new and serious long-term handicap. The "new leadership" in the National Committee and Congress did not include *one* new moderate or liberal Republican face. In fact, the Goldwater conservatives had made important gains in the House. With Laird in control of the Conference, and Rhodes as head of the Policy Committee, they had an even stronger power base than they had had prior to November. They would find it very useful in 1966 and 1968. The heavily pro-Goldwater staff of the Congressional Campaign Committee was not even touched in the shake-up. Here as elsewhere, the moderates had not begun to do the necessary house-cleaning.

But many moderates felt they had succeeded; they had unseated Burch. As they demobilized their forces and returned to their own states, the word went out from moderate leaders—"Give Ray Bliss a chance. Let's not complicate his job." The time for revolution had passed. Orthodoxy would now attempt to restore the Republican party.

The GOP in 1965:
Is the Bliss Formula Enough?

Veterans of the Washington press corps, on hand in Chicago for the National Committee meeting at which Ray Bliss became Chairman, spoke of "the end of the Goldwater era" in the Republican party. Nearly everyone present at this historic January gathering breathed a sigh of relief as the shy, bespectacled, smiling Ohio state chairman gave his brief acceptance speech. One hope, one attitude seemed to permeate the room. "If anyone can put the party back into working order, it's Mr. Bliss." Most everyone acknowledged the job was of enormous proportions but they quickly put out of mind any lingering doubts or qualms they might have

had. Bliss had done very well in Ohio, hadn't he? Comforting themselves with the wisdom of their choice they handed the wreckage
of the Republican party to their new leader, promised their cooperation and went home.

In the months since January, 1965, the new National Chairman
has applied himself indefatigably to his job. He expects long hours
from members of his staff. He has accomplished many short-term
goals and has done many things well. But what are Ray Bliss's
answers to the *long-range* problems he has inherited? What are
his chances for success in this area?

The Bliss formula for the Republican party, in a nutshell, has
been to apply the Ohio program nationally. In Ohio, Bliss maintained party unity through two techniques. First, he had the uni-
fying discipline of a strong Republican State Finance Committee—a
tightly controlled fund-raising mechanism. And in politics as elsewhere money is the key resource for maintaining control of an
organization. Second, he diverted the party's attention from ideological strife, concentrating it instead on organization and precinct
politics. He maintained a formal position of ideological neutrality
between candidates and factions.

The Bliss formula seeks to maintain an uneasy truce between
the Goldwater and moderate Republicans. In theory it would allow
time for wounds to heal, candidates to develop and Republicans
to win. It is sound "organization" politics. But is it enough for the
Republican party in 1966? We don't think that, by itself, it is—
for several important reasons.

1. *The Republican party is a party without "direction."* The
formula says nothing about which direction the Republican party
should take. It says nothing about "moving" at all. It is essentially
a formula for balancing, adjusting, and establishing equilibrium.
But the Goldwater experience has created a need for something
more. The Goldwater movement, the southern strategy, the radical
right—all of these were rooted in fundamental questions about the
direction of the Republican party. November, 1964, settled the
issue of direction for America (at least in negating the Goldwater
"choice") but *by itself* it could not settle this issue for the Republican party. The zeal with which the "new" conservatives have tried
to steer the party in very new directions is a brand new factor on
the current political scene. Most of the organization politicians
never understood this in 1963 and 1964. Many of them don't
understand this today.

2. *Unity is not the* ONLY *key to Republican success.* The current
strategy is to present a "united Republican front" accommodating all
shades of party opinion. The only real policy voice of the official
party is the Republican Coordinating Committee which reflects this

emphasis. It is composed of past presidential candidates and representatives of the Governors, State Legislators, the Congress, and the National Committee. A large and diffuse group, it has not often been able to speak with a voice which is both united and compelling.

One exception came at the first meeting in March of 1965, when, to the surprise of those who expected congressional conservatives to control the group, courageous Governor Thomas E. Dewey led a move that substituted a strong civil rights statement for the empty proposals made by the congressional leadership. But this episode does not yet appear to have set a precedent. Moreover, the several policy task forces which serve the RCC are ideologically balanced to the point where real creativity is stymied. Many Goldwater braintrusters are in the group; there are few new young faces, few "reformers," few "ethnic interest" leaders, and few young "academics" who have produced exciting ideas in recent years. The search for unity has become a quest for safety. An overemphasis on unity can produce a de-emphasis on creativity.

Republican moderates have always stood for an *inclusive* party and have criticized the "exclusionary" tactics of the 1964 campaign. This is a basic law in American party politics. As representatives of the majority of Republican voters, moderates believe that their policies will help produce the meaningful unity which the party needs. But unity—which was the keynote of most Republican leaders in 1965—is *not sufficient* for the Republican party today. There is a time for unity and a time for expressing differences in party affairs. Now there should be room for open and incisive debate on vital questions of philosophy and direction. For *now* is the time that Republicans must decide what appeals they will make in the elections of 1966, 1968, and 1972—times when unity will be expected and accorded.

Unity then is not *the* sole Republican answer. Unity tends to consolidate the existing base of the party and a unified minority is still a minority. Unity tends to be more concerned with keeping the far right in the party—at all costs—than with winning back the millions who did not feel at home with Republicanism in 1964. Unity is concerned with the present. It probes neither the past for understanding nor the future for direction. Unity rewards the lowest common denominator in the realm of ideas; it alone cannot generate enthusiasm or excitement for what is new and daring. Unity confirms power and discourages initiative. It is a virtue but it is not necessarily *the* virtue that will best direct the Republican party in the post-1964 political world.

3. *The organization formula has not prevented dissension.* For a moment the Republican party appeared to be united. Every top leader in the party approved the new order. Less than six months

after Chicago, however, Barry Goldwater formally launched his Free Society Association—the first serious indication that all was not well with the reconciliation approach. The American Conservative Union and the United Republicans of America have launched strong attacks on what they call the "liberal" takeover under Mr. Bliss.

The significance of this trend is clear. First, the conservative right can undercut a good part of the financial base of the Republican National Committee. The Free Society Association can raise big money. Its officers have spoken in terms of a 2.5 million dollar budget. Such plans go to the "jugular" of the Bliss formula—centralized financial control. Chairman Bliss has been working hard with his new Finance Chairman, General Lucius Clay, to pull together Republican fund-raising efforts. He has made some progress as, for example, with the congressional Boosters Club. But his chances for integrating right-wing money have been imperiled.

Moreover, groups like the Free Society Association that try to recruit a mass membership are fast becoming the command post for regrouping the conservative faction within the GOP. While pledging party loyalty, the FSA newsletter has attacked both major parties for failing to offer "a real political choice." The language is all too familiar to those who remember the Goldwater primary campaigns.

Meanwhile, some moderate Republicans have begun to grow impatient. But moderate Republican organizations (such as Republicans For Progress and other groups belonging to the Council of Republican organizations) are not a financial threat to the National Committee. They are not mass-membership organizations; they do not project large budgets and will not drain money away from the national treasury. The importance of these groups on the Republican left *and in the American center* is that they can provide the Republican party with the means for understanding new ideas and new people. They are the "cutting edge" through which the party can move back into the mainstream of American politics. Some conservatives say that the moderate activists are "irregular." What an ironic indictment! If the Republican regulars had been awake to their responsibilities for leadership in 1964 the GOP would not have conducted one of the most irregular, ideological, nonpolitical campaigns in American political history. What is so irregular in moving back to the political center, in asking amnesty for Republican defectors, in winning new votes from among Independents and Democrats, in making the Republican party exciting once again—concerned with people and the politics of a new generation? This is the strength of the Republican moderates. They hold the key to the center of American politics.

They are bridges across which new ideas, new energy, and new talent are moving into the Grand Old Party. From their ranks must eventually come the leaders of resurgent Republicanism.

Yet there is a danger that the party might lose this enthusiasm and fresh thinking of the middle. There must be more encouragement for moderate enthusiasts. They have, of course, been accepted in 1965 as a part of the ideological spectrum—a vast improvement over late 1964. But because they have less money and smaller organizational capabilities they often get less attention. At best they are another "interest group" with limited influence in the new articulation of a relevant Republican philosophy. Too often unity still demands that conflict over ideas be subdued.

Chairman Bliss, and the official party leadership, may well be doing all that they can at this point to revitalize the GOP. Our only concern is that our leaders be aware, as we are, that a great dilemma faces our party.

The GOP cannot regenerate and rebuild itself without making an unapologetic commitment to the center of American politics. But the Republican party can never win the center of American politics unless it assigns the major responsibilities for leadership to dynamic Republican moderates. There are many Republicans who shy away from these conclusions. Meanwhile the Republican party waits to see if it can work the miracle of organization without ideology.

But American politics will not wait. The pace of change is bewildering to Democrats as well as Republicans. Both parties prefer to think more about where they have been than about where they are going. If Republicans are to change this habit they must officially encourage and utilize the kind of thinking which can grasp the problems and policies of tomorrow.

This, then, is the next question we must face: What opportunities will the politics of the future hold for a new Republican party?

5

The Courage to
Embrace Tomorrow:

The "New Politics" and A New Republican Party

THE PRESIDENTIAL election of 1964 and its after-
math, President Johnson's continued popularity and the partial success of his "consensus politics," have obscured one central fact:
America stands on the verge of an exciting new era of politics.
Events are fast outracing the leaders of both major parties. A new
order is coming in American politics—based upon a new generation
and continued growth and concentration of population. By 1975, the
politics of today will be almost unrecognizable—in style, in vocabulary, and in substance. But few politicians have yet begun to
explore the changes which lie ahead. How will the new politics
affect the two-party system? What issues will dominate? Who will
lead the new order? And what impact will these changes have on
the lives of every American?

Few would pretend to answer these questions. Only a handful
of political seers have begun to examine the political scene of
tomorrow. They include scholars and journalists on the edge of
contemporary politics—men like pollster and writer Samuel Lub-
bell, management consultant Peter Drucker, and *Fortune* magazine
author Max Ways. In this chapter we shall suggest some new ideas
that may provide the raw materials for the new politics. And we
shall look at their implications for a new Republican party and a
winning Republican strategy.

The Passing of the Old Era:
The Crumbling Political Edifice

The current mood of American politics has a strange unreality
about it. Republican "rebuilding," now underway for some months,
has begun to restore a sense of "politics as usual." The Great
Society makes steady legislative progress against disorganized and
unconvincing opposition. An indefinite era of Democratic pre-

95

dominance is forecast by some journalists. Republicans want to forget Barry Goldwater. Many Democrats have begun to forget John F. Kennedy and Adlai Stevenson. Lyndon B. Johnson remains—the dominant political force, the great unifier of past with present.

But when we compare our political parties with virtually any other organization or institution in American society, we see how deceptive appearance is. By almost any standard of measurement our political parties and their leadership show the greatest lag in adjustment to change. American business and industry is rapidly adjusting to the revolution in data processing and automation. The entrepreneurial skills of the private sector are meeting the challenges of new, affluent and expanding markets. The situation today is the reverse of that which existed at the beginning of this century, when a great flood of national legislation was necessary to force American business to update its methods. The oldest institutions of the republic—the universities and the churches are experiencing an unprecedented ferment of innovation and reform.

In the political sphere a combination of fate and circumstance has somehow held back the forces of change. The Johnson consensus masks revolutionary change, change that was foreshadowed in the Kennedy years. In the early 1960s, the young Democratic President represented something new in American politics. The words of his inaugural address cut across the lines of party and spoke to a new and yet untried political force. "Let the word go forth from this time and place, to friend and foe alike, that the torch has been passed to a new generation of Americans. . . ." We in the Ripon Society, and young Americans generally, remember the challenge of this call. Yet today that torch burns only at an Arlington grave, for today no man and no party carries the torch of our generation.

This is the tragedy of 1964 and of our current politics. In the past campaign, what might have been a great debate became for the American people a grand detour. For the Republican party it was a dead end. The overbearing presence of a dominant political personality now prolongs our distraction from the politics of tomorrow. And the Republican party of the past, presented with rare opportunities to assert strong political leadership for the future, has only underlined its fundamental inability to understand or come to terms with the new America. At a time when the Republican party needs to be shaken from its foundations, challenged, renewed and rejuvenated, it has chosen instead the "safe" organizational solution. For this is the era of the caretaker politicians.

While Republicans "organize" to do battle on the old political terrain with increasingly obsolete weapons, events are already overtaking them. In the Congress, the long southern dominance of the

Senate is coming to an end. Scores of years of southern Democratic seniority in the House of Representatives have been lost as the one-party South has begun to crack. The Voting Rights Act and Negro registration drive make inevitable a recasting of party competition in the South.

Within the Democratic congressional party, the rise of the Democratic Study Group (a coalition of liberal and moderate House Democrats to which about half of the Democratic representatives belong), after years of careful planning and slow building, is a new and powerful factor in party politics. It is only a matter of time before this "new breed" challenges the Democratic old guard. Generational politics—the division along lines of age and seniority rather than party—has already been felt in some congressional votes, such as the Senate poll tax amendment to the voting rights bill. It was a factor in the Republican leadership fights of 1963 and 1965 that thrust "modern image" Republican Congressman Gerald Ford into the office of House Minority Leader.

Reapportionment—its full impact still to be felt in the Congress —will further recast the lines of party competition and draw ever newer and younger faces into contests for public office.

Yet our parties have not really begun to adapt to the new politics that threaten their very obsolescence. We have discussed at some length Republican efforts to "rebuild" after November 1964. Our general conclusion is that the "organizational" strategy avoids the real problems and opportunities for leadership. It is unlikely to redeem the massive Republican defections of 1964. It is even less likely to seize the "issue initiative" that could capture broad new support in the growing sectors of the voting population.

Nor can the Democrats take much comfort from their situation. When a majority party that has had almost unchallenged control of Congress for as far back as most young voters can remember does not speak to the future in a significant presidential campaign, it cannot build confidence in its capacity to lead. The phenomenon of the "teach-in" debates on American foreign policy is only one indication of the inability of a decaying party sytem to provide a forum for meaningful debate.

Why have our leaders not spoken to the needs of the new America? They have asked for ideas but they do not seem to be really interested in the problems that concern or excite the new generation. They speak another language, content to project their own picture of reality to an audience they do not understand. They speak without communicating. Their political braintrusts and research staffs and policy task forces go through the motions, but their position papers convince few. Little that is exciting or controversial survives committee government under the rule of the lowest common denominator. New ideas fail to break through into the old politics. Too many leaders fear the ideas which will challenge the conventional wisdom and comfortable clichés of the present, and thus their speeches and platforms and slogans and pamphlets do not ring true. Nor do they even begin to realize it. Already the dialogue of the 1966 congressional campaign has begun in the predictable monotones, the dull vocabulary of the past.

We believe that a *new* order is coming in American politics. With the end of the Johnson years the last link to the depression and war years will also be cut.

But who then will lead the new order? We would suggest that the future leaders of the Republican party, and perhaps the Democratic party as well, are largely unknown—that the lesson of 1964 was that Republicans must look to the future for their leadership. For those who were found wanting in the past cannot be adequate to the needs of the future.

Many Republicans compare the platform of 1964 with that of 1960—but not with the demands of a changing world. They still look to the leaders of the pre-Goldwater era—but not to new faces emerging in the states and in Congress. But history will not wait for the Republican party. By the mid-1970s the chances are that none of us will be able to recognize either of our great political organizations.

The Coming Political Era:
The Issues for a New Politics

Senator Everett Dirksen of Illinois, Republican Senate Minority Leader, when asked why he supported the 1964 civil rights legislation, replied: "Nothing is more powerful than an idea whose time has come." But even more important than an idea whose time has come is the idea whose time is yet to come. The political party that takes such ideas and makes them its own captures the future.

What are the issues of the future? What revolutionary changes will determine the dialogue of the new politics? Basically they are associated with the coming of age of a new generation that is unlike recent generations. It is a generation born in the depression, and war, and postwar years. It is a generation that does not remember or identify with the great issues that have divided Democrats and Republicans since the time of Franklin D. Roosevelt. The old economic issues are out of date. The new generation assumes and hardly stops to question a growing, abundant economy (though they worry about pockets of poverty), the basic social services of the American version of the welfare state, the right of trade union organization, equal rights for all Americans, and American leadership of the free world. Millions of its younger members, now flooding the universities and graduate schools of the nation, hardly remember Joseph Stalin, Senator McCarthy, Korea, Taft, or Churchill. This is largely a "have" generation, educated, affluent, expecting much from life. It is a generation whose outlook will place new demands on the American party system. Its current and most vivid impression of the Republican party is Barry Goldwater. It remembers John F. Kennedy and cannot quite believe in Lyndon Johnson. It is waiting, searching for something it does not yet see. It is eager, receptive.

When Franklin Roosevelt introduced the New Deal, the population of the United States stood at about 125 million. In 1960 it had grown to 180 million and by 1985 it will reach 275 million. The median age of our population, which has held at 29.5 years since 1940, will drop to 26.5 years in 1970. By the mid-1980s half of our population will be under twenty-five! Before the presidential election of 1972 we shall have become the youngest country in the West. And with this dramatic drop in the age of the population the political center of gravity will shift decisively to the new political generation.

Other trends besides population will shape the new politics. White-collar workers—including managers, sales, professional, and clerical workers—will comprise an increasing share of the working population. Already they have expanded from 29 percent of the work force in 1930 to 45 percent in 1964. The growing sector of professional and semi-professional employees will mean a steady disengagement from the older economic concerns and from the class polarization of management against labor. Educational opportunity will continue to expand. Since 1900 the number of college graduates in the United States has increased *six times* as fast as our population. Today almost half of those of college age go on for higher education and the proportion may soon increase to at least 70 percent.

Where will the new Americans live? In 1960, the Bureau of the Census located 63 percent of all Americans in 200 metropolitan areas (Standard Metropolitan Statistical Areas). These were not scattered across the country, but were instead largely grouped along three "Main Lines" each close to 500 miles long. One stretched from Boston to Washington, a second from Pittsburgh to Chicago, and a third from San Francisco to San Diego. The nine states that included the largest metropolitan complexes had together 80 million of the 1960 population of 180 million—about 44 percent of the total! During the 1950–1960 decade, population in the metropolitan areas grew by 26.4 percent and the nonmetropolitan population

only by 7.1 percent. We have not yet quite arrived at the phenomenon of the "super-city," or what social scientists call the "mega-
lopolis," but it is only a matter of time before the separate metropolitan areas begin to blend and merge into each other.

Already the political consequences of population concentration
are being felt. Regardless of how the reapportionment controversy
is resolved, the metropolitan complexes (including the suburbs *and*
the urban-core cities) will significantly increase their representation
in state and national legislatures. The gains will transform the
ground rules of party competition in several states. They will have
important effects on the kind of men and women who seek elective
office.

The nation's Governors, especially in the more populous states,
are already assuming a more active role in the national parties,
reversing a decline in party influence which culminated in 1960
when it seemed that the Governors had been replaced as "presidential timber" by members of the Senate. Interstate cooperation
in the solving of regional problems is growing. And as the states
prove their effectiveness in dealing with area problems without the
federal government, the prestige of state Governors is enhanced.

Even the South, which will continue to fall outside the belts of
the great super-cities, cannot escape the forces of urbanization.
Over the next decade or two these forces may well succeed in
breaking down the regional isolation of the South and reunifying
it with the economy and politics of the rest of the nation.

These are the basic dimensions of change. How will they be felt
in the issues of the new politics?

CIVIL RIGHTS: THE NEXT PHASE

Civil rights is the first new issue to rise to the surface of
domestic politics in the 1960s. The Republican party of 1964 came
down squarely on the wrong side of it. Republican members of
Congress can take much of the credit for passage of the 1964
Civil Rights Act. They provided political leadership far beyond
the promise of their numbers. Republican staff assistance—through
groups like the Republican Legislative Research Association—
played a key role in a coordinated congressional drive. But the
Republican party in writing its platform and in choosing its nominee
elected to ignore this congressional record and to fight instead with
a "Southern Strategy." The disastrous consequences for Republicans
at all levels have already been shown.

With the passage of the Voting Rights Bill in 1965, some observers began to speak of the end of the civil rights struggle.
The last great legal barriers will have been toppled, they point out,

and civil rights will cease to be a major political issue. How short-sighted a view! Can anyone in truth say that the American Negro's fight for equality is finished? The simple facts are that more Negroes are unemployed today than were a decade ago. The Negro unemployment rate is twice that of white workers and the gap is expanding. Among younger Negroes, one of the fastest growing sectors of the American population, unemployment is already an explosive problem, and many Negro jobs—at relatively low levels of skill—are most vulnerable to the real threat of automation.

Negro population continues to concentrate in the central core cities—New York, Philadelphia, Baltimore, Washington, Cleveland, St. Louis, Detroit, Chicago, Los Angeles—as the white flight to the suburbs increases. And with this trend the goals of adequate education and housing become more distant for most Negroes.

The civil rights movement is not just a Negro protest movement. It has drawn much of its support from progressive and responsible members of the white community. The dramatic involvement of the churches should long since have driven this point home to doubtful Republicans. The civil rights movement retains enormous political potential well beyond the numbers of the rapidly growing Negro electorate. And the concern of the movement will turn to the more subtle forms of discrimination—in education, employment, and housing—and to the vicious cycle of poverty in the urban ghettos. As Maine's Governor John H. Reed has said, "Like the metal shackles of slavery, the mental shackles of bigotry must be destroyed."

In a civil rights proclamation issued in July of 1965, the Council of Republican Organizations underscored the great tasks lying ahead. "The removal of legal barriers will not be enough," they said. "The Republican party is committed to equality—in reality— in all aspects of our Society." Then they went on to make a most telling point: "We know that the law is no more effective than the men who enforce it. Administrative performance and social performance must match legislative promise." All the good work Congress has done can be dissipated if the Department of Justice and the federal courts fail to implement the law adequately and fairly, or if personnel shortages cause considerable delays in the administration of justice. The CRO made specific recommendations for expediting judicial procedures.

The group—then composed of nine Republican organizations— also urged stepped-up enforcement of the Supreme Court school desegregation decision—and state and local action to correct racial imbalance in public schools. In Massachusetts the Republican Governor and Lieutenant Governor, John Volpe and Elliot Richardson, have undertaken important initiatives in this area. It is wide open for Republican leadership.

The group further suggested specific ways in which persistent discrimination in the field of housing, public accommodation, and public facilities and services can be ended. And in the area of employment opportunity it stressed how crucial it now is that Negroes be trained for jobs that the law has opened to them.* Much work must be done if civil rights is to mean more than the mere absence of legal barriers. Republicans ought to be doing it.

The American Negro still poses the most fundamental challenge to the workability of American democracy. While his fight for equal rights progresses, we will face some of the most critical years in our history. The problems of adjustment and acceptance will be painful and tense. They will call for responsible political leadership of the highest order. In 1964 the Republican party turned its face from this problem. The political temptation to do so again will increase—as white frustration and reaction build. To yield to them will be to fail both party and country.

HUMAN RIGHTS: THE FRINGE OF FREEDOM

But there is much more unfinished business for American democracy than the rights of the American Negro. Even now Republicans must look to the *next* phase in the struggle for human rights and dignity. We must now extend the concept of civil rights to all those who live on the fringe of freedom—to men and women who do not share the legal rights and civil liberties that we assume without question. These include the poor, and especially the poor with handicaps beyond mere poverty, such as the color of their skin, the language they speak, lack of education, or low intelligence.

Those called "mentally ill" comprise one such group of handicapped people. Ten percent of all the citizens in the Republic spend some time in mental institutions. Some 250,000 Americans are declared mentally ill each year. They occupy half of the nation's hospital beds. This is a sector of our population as large as our Negro population. But this problem *can* involve any American. Mental illness can reach into any family. Yet in many of our cities and states, the mentally ill are treated with less sympathy than criminals are—in asylums and in hospitals and in the courts. How

* See "A Republican Civil Rights Platform for 1965; A Statement of the Council of Republican Organizations. Prepared with the Assistance of the Ripon Society of Cambridge, Massachusetts," July 6, 1965.

See also "Republicans and Civil Rights: A Continuing Commitment." Published by the Critical Issues Council of the Republican Citizens Committee of the United States with research assistance from the Ripon Society, 1964.

is a person judged mentally ill? An incredible diversity of standards exists from state to state, from examiner to examiner. Some psychiatrists even consider political views in deciding whether men are insane—a familiar technique that is as objectionable in America as in countries where it has been employed as the tool of tyrants.

Americans must fight to guarantee the rights of all Americans who are the victims of personal or institutional injustice and discrimination. We must put aside the conventional wisdom about poverty and mental illness. We must champion individual dignity with understanding and compassion. A political party without a genuine social concern for others will not convince the new generation of Americans that it has a conscience. Those who enjoy rights must be convinced that those rights are not secure unless they are extended to everyone.

EDUCATION: FULFILLING THE AMERICAN DREAM

Education will be a central issue in the new politics. Our exploding population will create enormous education problems in the next twenty years. In the twenty-five year period between 1960 and 1985, the population will increase 50 percent! The school age population (5 to 24 years old) will skyrocket from 68 million in 1965, to 77 million in 1970, to 103 million in 1985! No wonder social analysts have started describing America as the Education State rather than the Welfare State.

Education has always been the road to the American dream. Already about half of our young men and women who complete high school go on to college. More and more American parents see a college degree as a passport to economic success or a ticket for social mobility for their children. As a result educators expect at least three million new college places to be added over the next decade! Students prolong their studies for graduate degrees to improve their choice of jobs and increase their options for the future. Graduate school enrollment is increasing 20 percent faster than college enrollment, and an estimated 80 percent of all Ivy League seniors go on to graduate studies. Education will soon surpass defense as America's largest single industry. Teachers are already our largest single occupational group.

Education will be an important political issue for several reasons. Educational spending forms a large and growing sector of all government budgets. State and local outlays for education alone have increased from 3 billion dollars at the end of the Second World War to 22 billion dollars last year—and budgets at these levels will more than *double* in the next seven years. But with this massive spending, public attention will shift to the quality and goals of education. For what purpose are we building ever more elaborate schools and great university complexes? Are we entering a new age of Social Darwinism on the American campus where the fittest survive and the losers are forgotten? Student protests this past year on our large university campuses—like those at Berkeley—have raised these haunting questions and challenged the familiar answers. Methods of education are coming under increasingly heavy fire. We are now beginning to taste the technological revolution that quantity education will force on us. Teaching techniques must undergo a drastic revolution. New ways of writing textbooks, team teaching, programmed learning, educational television must be evaluated and refined. The number of teachers per student will continue to decline, further upsetting traditional concepts of "the classroom." Three hundred thousand new college professors will be required in the next decade. Yet we graduated only 15,000 Ph.D.'s in 1965 and the rate cannot be expanded to keep pace with the demand.

Americans have too easily assumed that education is an end in itself. From our local school committees and Parent-Teachers Associations to our university boards of trustees and alumni associations, all Americans will have to rethink the purposes of our schools, colleges, and universities. What is taught and how it is taught are questions that the public has not yet begun seriously to debate.

But perhaps the deepest public concern with the educational system will stem from what some social critics have labeled the "diploma elite." There is a clear and present danger that formal educational qualifications—the mere possession of a college or graduate degree—may introduce new inequalities of opportunity in American society. Paper credentials may bear little relation to native ability or to the skills required for a particular job. Blue-collar and unskilled workers, Negroes and Puerto Ricans, may be denied access to jobs for which they are qualified. The uncritical American esteem for education may lead to new forms of discrimination and second-class citizenship. Lack of motivation, difficulties of speech and of understanding, poor home environment, are both an effect and a cause of de facto segregation. Diversity of educational standards is another problem. Unless state and local governments in a mobile society begin to coordinate their educational efforts voluntarily, the federal government will have to enforce national education standards as a condition of national survival.

The structure of the old politics is wholly inadequate for solving problems such as these. Forward-looking Republicans must begin to think and talk about the quality of education. We must be sensitive to the social consequences, in human terms, of the massive educational system we have so uncritically constructed. We can no longer deny that these are genuine topics of immediate political concern.

TECHNOLOGICAL CHANGE: NEW OPTIONS FOR THE PROGRESSIVE SPIRIT IN GOVERNMENT

The new era of politics will be an era of continued technological advance, abundance, and affluence. For most Americans advances in technology will mean increased possibilities to lead a fuller life. Some Americans, however, will not share in this abundance. The problems of poverty, inadequate education, and social and economic discrimination will gradually be recognized as interrelated and they will begin to yield to a coordinated attack.

The war on poverty and the Great Society are the Democratic party's answer to these problems. Far-reaching legislative and administrative changes are being introduced into the American welfare state by the Johnson Congress. It is safe to predict that these changes will produce a host of new issues. The federal government will be involved in complex decision-making far different from New Deal programs. The financing and coverage of the medicare program is just one example. Medical care, unlike payments of cash out of social security funds, involves services to the recipients and—inevitably—judgments by those who are administering the funds as to the worth and quality of those services. Who will make these decisions? Who will say what methods, treatments, and expenditures may be undertaken by private physicians in the treatment of a particular disease? Some doctors prefer one method, others prefer different methods of treatment for the same illness. There will be differences of cost and, no doubt, statistical variances in effectiveness. Eventually the government is likely to decree that one method rather than others should be used when treating a particular illness. Will doctors make these decisions or will accountants? Rigidity and timidity are both potential dangers in this area. Potential will become reality as government expenditure and control extend in the medical care field.

The sheer size of current Johnson Administration efforts is bound to result in some dramatic failures. Major administrative flaws have already been found in the war on poverty. Conflict between local leaders and politically appointed coordinators has threatened to scuttle many programs. Tomorrow's politics must try to institutionalize answers to these problems.

What is the Republican future in the Great Society? There is *no* future in calling for wholesale repeal of major items of Great Society legislation. Certainly there is room for responsible Republican criticism of the administrative failures. But progressive Republicans must themselves join in the search for sensible and efficient answers. The American people sense that the war on poverty, crime, disease, illness, and illiteracy is moving in the right direction. They will respect honest action more than poorly conceived and administered "legislative solutions" such as the rent subsidy bill, or mere negative partisan criticism.

But we can make no more important statement than this: *For Republicans, the real opportunities lie BEYOND the issue of "welfare state."* The technological revolution will afford Republicans new opportunities for humane and efficient reform in governmental bureaucracy and the public services. As the range of possibilities facing government decision makers expands, it will be more important than ever that we continually re-examine the decisions of the past. Are the assumptions upon which they have been based still valid? Can we find new and better ways to do the same job quicker and more economically?

Where they are appropriate, we should employ the most advanced technical administrative tools—computers, cost-benefit analysis, organization and method studies. Because new electronic computers can store enormous volumes of data in memory banks, they can be used to facilitate the individual treatment of each person on the basis of his special situation. Personalized treatment will become possible in the processing of social security benefits, income tax returns, and student and home-owner loans. The crude operation of today's impersonal bureaucracy can be made sensitive to the personal needs and requirements of every man and woman. The technological breakthrough in computer science means that individual freedom can be increased without contracting the freedom of others. Government can become more responsive.

It also means that tyranny can be tailor-made and extended to cover the minutiae of detail it never could in the past. A central data bank, in the hands of an unscrupulous and unchecked political elite, would be a short distance from the totalitarian controls of George Orwell's chilling *1984.* Already the electronic eavesdropping and recording devices used by American business and government, not to mention the more subtle invasions of privacy represented by much "psychological" testing, threaten to subvert the relationship of individuals and institutions. Can personal freedom be protected in such an age? The new technology will require new techniques of democratic control to insure that governmental power is used responsibly.

The Republican party has often been the party of progressive reform in government, and efficiency in the public services is a basic progressive theme. People want efficient government, efficient in spending their tax money *and* efficient in meeting and anticipating their needs. But new scientific and technical developments have changed the meaning of efficiency. The political party unable to move from the issues of the past runs the risk of becoming irrelevant to the concerns of the present. It most certainly forfeits the options of the future.

METROPOLITAN LIVING: THE QUALITY OF ENVIRONMENT

The growth of the super-city will pose political and economic challenges of a new order for American government. The new metropolitan areas of our country are scarcely governable today. The traditional forms of local, state, and federal government have not been able to keep pace with metropolitan growth. The new generation of educated and affluent Americans will find most of their jobs in the corporate and professional world of the super-cities. The new metropolis offers them the greatest possibilities for career advancement, the range of cultural life they have grown accustomed to and now demand, the educational and health facilities they want for their children. The new Americans are acutely aware of the environment in which they live—of its shortcomings, of the failures and successes of local and state governments in dealing with them. They want clean air and clean water. They want *enough* air and *enough* water. Day after day they experience the inadequacies and frustrations of metropolitan transportation. As a mobile generation, they are sensitive to the need for new air and highway safety programs. They know that a subterranean world of crime and violence may at any moment reach out to them and twist their lives. And in their more hopeful moments, at least, they suspect that it all does not have to be this way. They wait for answers—and they are willing to look to either political party.

The new generation of Americans finds it hard to understand the continued existence of widespread corruption in the governments that supposedly serve them. They fight for school bond issues and constitutional reform in their states. They are increasingly impatient with narrow and exclusive ethnic politics, with the patronage and boondoggling and payoffs of a passing era. They are looking for responsible political leadership.

In summary, new political demands will emerge at the points of greatest population concentration. The eternal struggle of man to master his environment will find its most difficult challenge in the jungles of tomorrow's super-cities.

THE REVOLUTION IN THE STATES AND LOCAL CITIES:
GOVERNMENT FOR TOMORROW

The future of state and local government will be an immediate problem of the new politics. Already state and local governments have expanded at an astonishing rate. For the past twenty years, while critics attacked "centralization of power" and the "enormous expansion of the federal government," the truly dynamic growth has come at the state, county, and municipal level. Since 1946, state and local expenditures have increased sixfold. In 1964, state and local governments spent a total of 64 billion dollars—*twice* as much as the federal government spent on domestic programs. And the pace will accelerate. Economists estimate state and local spending will reach $82 billion by 1967, $100–120 billion by 1970 and as much as $155 billion in 1974 as these governments assume greater responsibilities for education, health and sanitation programs, housing and community development.

The Republican party has a unique opportunity to meet the governmental needs of the future, for Republicans have historically been sympathetic to state initiative and responsibility. They have been less inclined than the Democrats to seek the solution of all problems through the federal government. Republicans understand that a "creative federalism" will require the mutual respect and cooperation of governments at all levels.

One problem that responsible Republican leadership will have to meet is the constant danger of "tax revolt." Today state and local budgets, bond issues, tax increases, etc., provide the average American with his only meaningful control on the level of government spending. The federal budget, measured in billions of dollars, has long since passed the comprehension of the American taxpayer. Public discontent with government spending bears most heavily on state and local units. But Republicans must avoid the easy route of encouraging public rebellion and stimulating tax revolt. Republicans have a special challenge in leading the American voter to an understanding of "state responsibilities," particularly in the realm of fiscal policy.

Republicans must face an immediate problem, rapidly approaching crisis proportions—the limited base of tax resources. As almost any taxpayer will attest, property taxes, sales taxes, and state income taxes have already reached or passed the limits of political feasibility in most of our larger states. Our Governors have, as a direct result, had an unusually high political mortality rate. The ordeal of finding new revenues for existing programs limits their ability to meet new needs.

What can be done to ease the fiscal crisis in states and localities? Taxes can be reformed and adjusted, credit can be strengthened and extended, federal aids can be reviewed and streamlined. But none of these options can give more than limited relief. Without more dramatic help it is likely that state functions will continue to slip away under the enormous pressures of the next two decades.

But our search for a "simpler and better way" is not without hope. For in dramatic contrast to the bleak fiscal picture at the local and state level, the federal government today faces the prospect of increasing revenues. Because the federal tax structure is highly responsive to economic growth, prosperity generates ever-increasing tax returns. There is expectation that these revenues will soon begin to exceed expenditures. Unless this margin is returned to the economy, observers fear it will act as an automatic "brake" on national growth. This concern helped to bring about the 1964 tax cut, but even that did not sufficiently limit "the federal suction machine."

In 1964 Presidential Advisor Walter Heller pointed to a 6 billion dollar annual increase in federal tax revenue and suggested that a part of it be funneled back into the economy through unrestricted grants to the states.

For a while it seemed as if everyone were for it. The White House supported the plan during the 1964 campaign. So did Senator Goldwater. Both party platforms gave it favorable notice. The Conference of State Governors supported it enthusiastically, as did a special presidential task force. But in December of 1964, President Johnson, angered at news leaks, abruptly shelved the proposal. It has been revived since then, in a joint study issued by the Republican Governors' Association and the Ripon Society in July of 1965* and in legislation filed in Congress by Republican legislators. A similar proposal for bloc grants to the states was also adopted by the Republican Coordinating Committee in December 1965. Such proposals deserve continued Republican attention.

At the same time, reforms are needed in our complicated, contradictory, and chaotic federal tax structure. Republicans can also take the lead in developing a stronger partnership with private enterprise at the state and local level—to tap the creative business process and to build a sound economic base for new industry and jobs.

Most important, sound state government will require constitu-

---

* "Government for Tomorrow. A Proposal for the Unconditional Sharing of Federal Tax Revenues with State and Local Governments." A research paper issued jointly by the Republican Governors' Association and the Ripon Society, July 1965.

tional reform and a strengthening of state legislatures. This is a wide open area for meaningful Republican action. Population concentration, reapportionment, out-dated administrative structures, the explosion of needs for services have all compounded the need for overdue constitutional revisions. But constitutional reform must be more than a re-evaluation of existing governments within state borders. It should also look toward techniques of cooperation with neighboring states that share a metropolitan complex or have common regional concerns. Moreover, the cause of constitutional reform offers Republicans a unique means for involving more citizens directly in problems of *their* government. Bold Republican leadership here could be an important step toward rebuilding the Republican party in the states.

Strengthening the state legislatures is a high priority challenge for the new politics. Most state legislatures do not enjoy a fraction of the professional staff available to Governors or administrative departments. The United States Congress has been far in advance of the states in attaining expert staff assistance. Even this year Congress is further evaluating and updating its internal organization. But the state legislator is the "forgotten man of American politics"—underpaid, understaffed, underpublicized, he cannot contribute his full weight to the solution of state political problems. His position must be improved. Coordination and exchange of information among state legislators should also be encouraged. The establishment of a Republican State Legislators' Association in August, 1965, under the chairmanship of Monte Montgomery, Speaker of the Oregon House, is an important step in that direction.

State and municipal government will be one of the most challenging frontiers of the new political era. We have not yet begun to assemble the political and administrative talent to meet these challenges. This we must do if we are to build good government for tomorrow. The new Republican leadership should pursue this goal. It is a great responsibility and a great opportunity.

AN INNOVATIVE FOREIGN POLICY

The contrast between the Kennedy and Johnson administrations is most dramatic in the area of foreign policy. After a relatively short time, the innovating spirit of the Kennedy administration has all but disappeared. The new initiatives of the Peace Corps, the Alliance for Progress, the limited test ban treaty, the AID concept, the new Atlantic Community, whatever their shortcomings, have had no counterparts under Johnson. There have been few "new departures." The Johnson approach has been a very personal, tough, no-nonsense foreign policy with wide public support. Yet there is an uneasiness everywhere and the beginnings of criticism from some academicians, writers, and church leaders. But this uneasiness has seldom been reflected in inter-party debate. Our parties, as such, have not been responsive to the real foreign policy issues that are exciting public controversy and interest.

As America moved from the Eisenhower to the Kennedy years, it experienced more than a change in ruling parties. It observed a change in political generations and in style of leadership, particularly in foreign affairs. The new style policy was not always accurate, not always consistent, not always effective. But its capacity for historical perspective and its sensitivity to the subtle dynamics of international relations began to accomplish limited but important results. It promised much more.

There is much to say in criticism of the President's foreign policy. Republicans, who have produced some of the nation's most alert and able diplomats, should be saying it. We dare not abandon the role of "opposition" to the irresponsible and unrealistic critics of the "new" radical left.

There is a continuing need today for that rare mixture of idealism firmly linked with a solid grasp of reality which has characterized the best of this nation's foreign policies. There is a need for a spirit that is patient with small steps because it sees their larger meaning. This was the spirit of the Kennedy Inaugural address, the spirit of "But let us begin." And there are places where this spirit can be put to work. We need, for example, a grand plan for harnessing the atom and restricting the proliferation of nuclear weapons. We must better share our bountiful harvests with those who lack sufficient food. The numbers who must be fed should be limited through an intensive international program of population control. There is a need for cooperation in the exploration of outer space. International student traffic has increasingly contributed to the cross-pollination of cultures, but it should be better systemized. Several years ago President Eisenhower suggested an international United Nations University. One should be created and with it a whole network of international universities using new and existing educational facilities in bold new ways. The new generation will respond to calls in these and other areas. But President Johnson has not sounded the trumpet.

Young America is waiting for a demonstration of leadership in foreign affairs. And it ranks foreign policy high among its potential concerns. Today the new generation of Americans finds little that recommends itself in the foreign policy leadership of *either* of our political parties.

A STRATEGY FOR REPUBLICANS:
   THE COURAGE TO ENTER THE NEW POLITICS

It is remarkable how slow our political parties have been to grasp some of the issues in the "new politics"—how unwilling to adapt to the new political environment. We believe that this gap provides the best opportunity for a *new* Republican party. But ideas are not patentable, and if the Republican party does not seize them, the Democratic party will. This is the immediate challenge to thoughtful Republicans.

What strategy, then, for Republicans? As Mrs. Clare Boothe Luce has suggested, Republicans must *leap-frog* the Democrats into the isues of the future. They must leave behind the meaningless arguments of conservatism versus liberalism, public versus private, business versus labor, hard line versus soft line, and come to terms with the really new challenges. Republicans, not burdened with administrative responsibility for the present, are in a position more objectively to judge and more freely to reach out to these opportunities. If we truly are to honor our yesterdays then we must grasp our tomorrows.

Republicans, if they are to have a future, must "go hunting where the ducks are" as they look for support. They must go where the new voters *are* and compete for their support. Meaningful competition for these voters in terms of the new issues has hardly begun. How sad, with such an opportunity untapped, that some Republicans should seek and applaud an increase in their numbers from the ranks of discredited southern Democrats. Unable or unwilling to win in the present and the future, Republican leaders in 1965 have settled for the trophies of the past, a few discarded "white elephants."

The growth areas that Republicans must tap are not obscure. Geographically they are in the expanding urban centers and suburbs of the North and West and among the Negroes of the deep South. Economically they are America's burgeoning middle class. Occupationally they include the huge new numbers of college graduates, the new business and professional class, the employees of service industries. The trainees of the service industries already represent the greatest occupational growth area in America. They are the men and women who install and program computers, who service dial telephones, color television sets, and complicated auto transmissions. They are highly trained, continually updating their skills to maintain their jobs. They are can-do people caught up in the present; counterparts of the skilled workers who formed the backbone of the powerful Republican party at the turn of the century, under Mark Hanna, William McKinley, and Theodore Roosevelt.

But modern Republicans have not been good political strategists. They have used little of the creative genius or entrepreneurial skill of the business community and the private sector. They have been more like a stockholder afraid to make investments for the future. Their portfolios have come to include only stocks that are on the wane, past their peak. They have watched a rising market pass them by. They have remained the corner grocery store in the day of the supermarket.

When they have had the daring to invest, they have fallen ready prey to the easy money schemes. They have been bewitched by the flash in the pan, by short run gains and short-sighted strategies—the anti-communism of McCarthy, the anti-labor crusade of "right-to-work," the patent medicines of the radical right, the southern strategies of 1964.

The lessons are obvious, Republicans must invest in groups with a future, groups on the way up. Republicans must reach out and touch these concerns. We must fight for the interests of Negroes, of the youth, of the middle-class suburbanite, and of the new sophisticated technician, for these are the people who will shape America's political future.

Without *them* the Republican party has *no* future.

THE FINAL PRESCRIPTION:
THE INITIATIVE TO LEADERSHIP

The strategy for a new Republican party is clear. All that the Republican party needs now is the leadership to implement it. But the lessons of 1964 and 1965 demonstrate the failure of leadership. The Republican party has yet to find the men and women who can speak to the political concerns of the new America. We need men and women who are not afraid to innovate, to make the bold move, the dramatic appeal. The Republican party needs, in short, the *initiative to leadership.*

The Bible warns men not to put "new wine into old bottles"—"else the bottles break, and the wine runneth out, and the bottles perish." If men put new wine into new bottles both will be preserved. The bottles of the Republican party are growing old. They have been taped and retaped by a caretaker leadership. They bespeak a great weariness. Yet the effort goes on to use them one more time. The caretakers may be fooled but the people will not. The wine is a new vintage and it is only a matter of time before the bottles burst.

Where then will the Republican party find this new leadership?

Some of it will come from the younger ranks of Republican Governors and Congressmen. But if these men do not soon develop the boldness to break with the past, history will pass them by as well. At a time when the future is still open, the Republican party needs more men with the courage to win, more men who will stand up and be counted, men who see the future for what it is. We believe that men will look back on the Convention of San Francisco as a great divide in Republican politics. For there men stood alone and were judged as individuals. That crucible separated steel from dross. The qualities of leadership that America saw and admired in those hours will survive the new era of politics. The Republicans who will rebuild their party as an instrument of the future will be men and women largely unknown to the politics of 1964, but men and women who share the purpose, the courage, and the vision of those Republicans who found their noblest hours in pulling against a current that was flowing into the past.

These new leaders of the Republican party will find their greatest opportunity for growth and recognition in the states rather than the Congress. Democratic party inattention to state and local government will afford Republicans a chance for exciting political leadership. Political competition at the state level will be more evenly based. Reapportionment will insure new chances to contest state legislative seats and to recruit new candidates for the Republican ticket.

The new political role of the Republican Governors is one of the few bright developments in the Republican party, yet even here the potential has hardly been realized. The Republican Governors and for that matter the Republican State Chairmen represent the real hope for a new Republican party. They are on the frontiers of policy, participants in the most dynamic sector of American government, afforded the widest range for political leadership. They are closer to the problems and concerns of a growing population. They have fielded winning teams and winning platforms. They are *the* Republican success story, yet many national leaders have not grasped the significance of this fact. Senator Goldwater has attacked the Republican Governors' Association as a divisive moderate "splinter group."

Republican leaders in the states must begin to communicate with each other, to exchange ideas and strategies. The Republican Governors, state Attorneys General, labor commissioners, and other department heads should meet together nationally and regionally as most of these groups already do on a nonpartisan basis. We can no longer afford to compartmentalize some of the greatest resources available to the Republican party.

The new Republicans must organize liaison among young state

legislators and among Republican mayors, and the Association of Republican County Chairmen should become more than a polling organization. In sum, the combined levels of Republican organization within and among the states provide Republicans with their greatest hope for rebuilding a new party.

A new generation is coming to power in the Grand Old Party. It is already beginning to reshape and rebuild that party so that it may live a useful and successful political life. It is not easy to trust the young and inexperienced with leadership. Many wondered when they took command whether they would succeed in 1776, in 1860, in 1900, in 1960. Yet the burden of the future will always rest on the shoulders of young men and women. From this generation must now come the leaders of our party and our country. The burden is theirs, and the honor.

6

THE KEY TO VICTORY

> Had we world enough, and
> time
> Your coyness, lady, were no
> crime.*

TOO OFTEN responsible Republicans have resembled the coy lady when talk has turned to action. They ignore the harsh truth that the time to do something about the condition of the party is now! We have not world enough nor time to wait. Republican moderates now bear a heavy and inescapable responsibility to guide their party. To fail at this moment will jeopardize not only the survival of a broadly based Republican party but also the very political health of the American nation. No matter how we may try to escape the unpleasantness of contemporary Republican politics, we cannot escape the judgment of history.

We believe that the key to Republican victory lies in a three-fold commitment. Responsible Republicans must articulate a vital moderate Republican philosophy, they must participate more actively in Republican politics, and they must achieve a long term plan of moderate Republican action. But to succeed, moderates must be "more than moderate" in their commitment. The Republican party needs more activists, more pamphleteers, and more "revolutionaries" of the *center* if it is to keep its mind and soul from falling captive to extremist movements in American politics.

Responsible Republicans have been guilty of one *false* assumption that may all too soon become a *fatal* assumption. They have shared a naive optimism, a distant unconcern, an assumption that political parties will take care of themselves. Having won the presidency in 1952 and 1956, moderate Republicans paid little attention to the grass roots of Republicanism, to the need for mature policy discussion, or to the task of building a strong organization. Barry Goldwater and the "conservative" movement were the stepchildren of this inattention. The presidential campaign of 1964 should have taught all thoughtful Americans this—that when

---

* Andrew Marvel, "To His Coy Mistress."

116

one of our political parties forsakes moderate leadership, all Americans must share the cost.

The responsibility is today even greater. For a weakened Republican party, under "nonideological" leadership and confronted by a strengthened "conservative" cadre is in far greater danger if responsible Republicans do not lead!

The Courage to Believe:
A Moderate Manifesto

In 1964, the Republican party adopted a "conservative" ideological stance—with unhappy results. A Republican philosophy that will capture the imagination of the American people must have at least three attributes. It must be oriented toward the solution of the major problems of our era—it must be "pragmatic" in emphasis. It must also be "moderate" in its methods—concerned more with the complexities of methods than with a simplistic view of ends. And finally, it must marry these attributes of pragmatism and moderation with a passion to get on with the tasks at hand.

First, our philosophy must be oriented toward the solution of problems. The image of "negativism" that has too frequently been attached to our party must be dispelled. The new generation in American politics is looking for a party that is able to grasp the realities of its world, that exhibits a sensitivity to the problems that are its concern. This means that the first task of the Republican party is to wake up to the problems of the last half of the twentieth century.

Vision is a recognition of problems; it is a function of leadership. The Republican party has produced a proud lineage of pragmatic statesmen since Lincoln. It is our hope that once again it will provide the leadership to meet the challenges we have outlined: in civil and human rights, education, urban concentration, governmental reform, strengthening state and local government, and in developing a creative foreign policy.

While our philosophy and our program must be pragmatic so must they be moderate. Simply to define the problems is not to solve them. The moderate recognizes that there are a variety of means available to him, but there are no simple, unambiguous ends. He recognizes hundreds of desirable social goals where the extremist may see only a few. The moderate realizes not only that ends compete with one another, but that they are inextricably related to the means adopted for their pursuit. He often sets proximate goals, and he gives disciplined attention to the problem of technique. The moderate chooses the center—the middle road—not because it is half way between left and right. He is more than a nonextremist. He takes this course since it offers him the greatest possibility for constructive achievement. And he does all of this, not because he lacks ideals, but because he is passionately concerned with realizing them.

In contrast, the extremist rejects the complexity of the moderate's world. His is a state of mind that insists on dividing reality into two antithetical halves. The gray is resolved into black and white. Men are either good or evil. Republicans are either liberal or conservative. It is understandable that the incredible complexity and mounting frustrations of our world will cause men to seek one right answer—the simple solution. The moderate cries out that such solutions do not exist, but his would appear to be a thankless task. Who will reward him for telling them their dreams can never be? It is not surprising that the doctrinaire has always reserved his greatest scorn for the pragmatist. The moderate poses the greatest danger to the extremist because he holds the truth that there is no absolute "truth" that can make the complexities of man and his society simple. There is no escape from reality—most certainly not in the realm of political life.

Moderation is not a full-blown philosophy proclaiming the answers to all our problems. It is rather a point of view, a plea for political sophistication, for a certain skepticism to "total" solutions. The moderate has the audacity to be adaptable, to seek the specific solutions most appropriate to the needs of his nation. The Republican moderate approaches these problems from a more conservative perspective, the Democratic moderate from a more liberal one. The fact that we may meet on common ground is not "me-tooism." It is time to put away the tired old notion that to be "real Republicans" we must be as different as possible from our opponents! There is no more sense in that view than in the idea that we must be for isolationism, prohibition, or free love because our opponents are not. It is time we examined solutions on their own merits rather than set our policy simply in terms of the position the Democratic party may have taken. If we let the Democrats preempt good positions on every issue while we simply react— then we are doomed to continuing futility.

But can the moderate produce the image of conviction and dedication that has been so much a part of the attraction of extremists throughout history? Is the "flaming moderate" just a joke, or does he represent a viable political mood? Can we be emotional about a politics so pluralistic, so relative, so realistic in defining the available range for maneuver? Perhaps we are possessed by a too abundant enthusiasm, but we feel not only that we can— but also that we must. We must show our world that emotion can be aroused by a purpose more noble and a challenge more universal than the cries of the irresponsible extremist. Tempered with an honest uncertainty, we must be ever willing to enter upon yet another great crusade. We must learn to be as excited about open-mindedness as we once were about final answers, as dedicated to partial solutions as we have been to panaceas. We must engage life as we find it, boldly and courageously, with the conviction that if reason endures we shall surely succeed—and with the knowledge that the greatest sin is not to have fought at all.

The Courage to Work:
A Call to Action

Early in his political career, while he was still a Congressman, Abraham Lincoln wrote William H. Herndon, his Springfield, Illinois, law partner:

> Now as to the young men. You must not wait to be brought forward by the older men. For instance do you suppose that I should ever have got into notice if I had waited to be hunted up and pushed forward by the older men. You young men get together and form a Rough & Ready club, and have regular meetings and speeches. Take in every body that you can get, Harrison Grimsley, Z.A. Enos, Lee Kimball, and C.W. Matheny will do well to begin the thing, but as you go along, gather up all the shrewd wild boys about town, whether just of age or little under age—Chris Logan, Reddick Ridgely, Lewis Zwizler, and hundreds such. Let every one play the part he can play best—some speak, some sing, and all holler. Your meetings will be of evenings; the older men, and the women will go to hear you; so that it will not only contribute to the election of "Old Zach" but will be an interesting pastime, and improving to the intellectual faculties of all engaged. Don't fail to do this.

We believe that Lincoln also wrote that letter to us. We will not wait to be "brought forward by the older men" any more than he did. We too want to speak and sing and holler. And as we do, we also want to gather up "all the shrewd wild boys about town" to join us in meeting the great challenges and opportunities which face our generation.

The need for individual participation in politics is just as pressing as it was in Lincoln's time, but much more possible for the average citizen. The leisure age is upon us and sages wring their hands and shake their heads as they wonder what people will do with all their free time. The campaign of 1964 suggests that we have not devoted *enough* time to our politics. Citizens must devote more time to study and to political action. As ever larger percentages of our population join the leisure class we face a tremendous opportunity and responsibility for achieving a new golden age of democracy.

The coming era can challenge the best in us. Moderates can use their increased time and money as effectively as have the extremists. If they do they will learn that politics can be fun; that their participation can be meaningful. We can all become "happy warriors."

Many moderates throw up their hands, saying that modern politics is a "dirty business" and they want nothing of it. Yet these same people look in horror on the Goldwater nomination and condemn party leaders for failure to apprehend the nature of the right-wing movement within the Republican party. Politics always has been "dirty," and to the extent this is true the blame lies solely with the citizen who would rather complain about the mess than handle the mop. Can we expect men of high caliber to run for office when the public views their participation as inherently corrupt? By the same token, can we expect the Republican party to face national problems realistically, when the vast majority of its members leave the field of policy formation to activists of more extreme views? The active participation of moderates is essential to the growth and responsibility of the Republican party.

Where can a moderate Republican citizen begin? What can you do to help rebuild the Republican party, right now? Some answers are fairly obvious.

You can become better acquainted with the local political scene. Attend local Republican meetings and be certain to enroll formally as a member. Watch for indications of what the leadership is thinking. Let them know how you feel; as a member you have at least some bit of leverage. Your leader retains his power by keeping people like you happy. Speak for what you believe in. Make your own proposals and solicit support for them. Bring like-minded friends into the organization.

Make yourself known to fellow moderates—a key point. Often a few extremists are able to take over an organization or dominate a meeting because each moderate thought he stood alone though in reality he was a part of an undiscovered majority. Don't doubt your capacity to make an impact on events. Be proud of your views; pursue your own objectives. Too many moderates keep peace by adjusting to the views of others. Let other people come over to your point of view for a change.

Support good candidates—with both money and manpower. Urge able community leaders to run for office and promote their candidacy in special interest groups of which you are a member. Take on the responsibilities of leadership yourself. Your influence is magnified when you represent others. A precinct captain can speak for a thousand or more voters in his bailiwick. Such positions often go begging for someone to fill them. Able citizens who are willing to put out some energy can quickly earn the right to influence others, the right to speak with authority.

Keep yourself informed on issues. Read carefully; clip and file useful materials. Become an "expert" in something. It takes surprisingly little effort to know more than your colleague about a given issue—and the man who knows a little more is indispensable. Knowledge is power. Form pools of knowledgeable people and make your services available to political figures. Join or support policy and research operations on the local and national level. Communicate your views to editors, commentators, party and government officials. If your opinion is well informed, if your position is well argued, it can be influential.

In all of this, remember that politics is a year 'round business. The elections—primary and general—are high points but their results are the products of the unpublicized ground work which preceded them. Local skirmishes, caucuses, and conventions are where you can best make your influence felt. But first you must dare to become involved. Moderates must make a genuine commitment to political action on the local level for this is the predecessor of effective national party leadership. Here lies the first testing ground for the future of moderate Republicanism.

The Courage to Win:
A Strategy for the Republican Party

Having survived the shock of the Goldwater experiment, the Republican party is in danger of becoming accustomed to losing. Yet if Republicans become reconciled to being second best, to being a permanent minority or loyal opposition, the new generation of American voters may not even accord them that consolation. Republicans must have the courage to win *now*. The key to Republican victory will lie in the work done *before* the presidential campaigns of 1968 and 1972.

We suggest now only the most important elements for a winning Republican strategy.

First and most important, the Republican party must attract the new generation of American voters, not just to swell the ranks of Republican voters, but, more significantly, to provide new sources of leadership and talent for the party. The new generation of Americans will define the issues of the new politics we have outlined. They can give the Republican party a new direction. If the party has not welcomed many of them by 1968 and 1972, it may well be too late.

Second, the liberals, moderates, and traditional conservatives of the Republican party must recognize their *common* interest—an interest thrown into sharp outline by the ultra-conservatism that triumphed within the party in 1964. The true conservatives of the Republican party must make a clear commitment to winning elections rather than the pursuit of a narrow ideology. Republicans must vigorously contest the center ground of American politics. They must recognize that organizational improvement is not enough if the party is to reset its direction and regain its momentum.

Third, responsible Republicans must work systematically to reclaim the Republican party organization from the precincts to the top levels of the national party organization. The danger of a minority faction keeping control of the party machinery has become a reality in state after state. Traditional Republicans must welcome new and younger blood in restoring the Republican machinery across the nation to a broadly representative status. It will not be enough just to replace one set of discredited faces with another.

Fourth, Republicans must start rebuilding in states with races for Governor, especially in 1966, and in the numerous state legislative elections brought about by the rapid trend of reapportionment. Today, some of the greatest talent in the Republican party resides in the state capitols and legislatures. As state parties are rebuilt, they will provide candidates for the United States Senate and House of Representatives. Republican control of state government is essential to provide some balance to the current Democratic monopoly at the federal level of government.

Fifth, Republicans must give high priority to fielding attractive moderate candidates for the House and Senate in 1966 and 1968. Republicans will be running against a popular President and a productive Congress, The new breed of young Democrats that has come to Congress in recent years will be astute competition. Republicans must put their best talent forward. An interim-platform or statement of Republican principles could be a big assist if Republican moderates are able to contribute their best to it.

Finally, Republican moderates must begin now to develop a coordinated strategy for the Republican National Convention of 1968. As San Francisco made plain the Goldwater takeover of the Republican party to millions of Americans who watched in disbelief, so the 1968 convention will bear witness to what the Republican party has or has not learned from the election of 1964. Moderates must early contest for seats as delegates and alternates to the convention. They must prepare a new Republican platform, broadly representative of Republican tradition and American aspirations. We must convince the American people that the Republican party has changed from 1964 and changed dramatically.

This, then, is a call to action. Let there be no mistake about that. The responsibilities of leadership have been neglected too often in the unhappy past. All of us must now respond to the challenges of the future. We must change the tone and content of contemporary Republicanism—and with it the nature of political debate in a rapidly changing America.

The question is often asked, "Where are the leaders of the new Republican party?" We have shown in this book just how much we need such men.

If we cannot find them, let us become them.

An Epilogue to the Reader:

Some Personal Reflections

THIS ACCOUNT of Republican politics is in many respects a diary and a testament—written by young men and women of the Ripon Society who took part in the actual events. We have tried to share with you some of the natural excitement we have felt—as it were—participating in history. At times events have outraced us, leaving us with the human frustration of impotence. At other times we have seen the impact that men and ideas can have in shaping the course of a political party. Always we have had a fascination with the endless variety of challenges and opportunities that is so much the attraction of politics.

A flourishing group of bright young Republicans in the Cambridge and Boston community—drawing important support from the faculties and graduate schools of Harvard, M.I.T., and Tufts—was bound to attract some attention. But the progress of the Ripon Society in Republican politics has had more basic roots. In the three years since it was founded, the Society has actively involved talented young people—from the universities, the professions, and business—in the art of practical politics. It has sought to complement ideas with action, to dispel the image of the Republican party as uninformed or anti-intellectual. Ripon members have worked in teams and as individuals on policy research, political analysis, and speech writing. The Society has welcomed as guests and speakers numerous Republicans of national stature—gaining the benefit of their perspective on politics—and sharing ours with them.

Today the Ripon commitment to the Republican party continues to grow. I am often asked, "What hope do you see in the Republican party?" "Why should I become a Republican?" Speaking as a committed Republican, I feel there are important reasons why young men and women should channel their energies, hopes, and idealism into the Republican party.

I share the growing belief of many young Americans that politics is one of the noblest human endeavors. The problems that confront our nation both in domestic and in foreign policy demand a quality of leadership that we have not found in either of our political parties. Our generation is no longer content with "politics as usual." It demands and expects more from both politics and public service. The Peace Corps and the civil rights movement illustrate this new and significant commitment. We believe that the Ripon Society represents a similar opportunity for commitment within the Republican party. The impoverishment of one of our great political parties can only hurt us all. We need to attract the best minds and talent to the Republican party as an essential part of the solution to the broader challenges that face America, whether they be the racial tensions of our growing urban ghettos or the difficult dilemmas of our commitment in Southeast Asia.

The Republican party presents the greatest political challenge facing young America. The work of rebuilding has hardly begun. There is a calling to a vital and expanding new generation to restore a once great party and to return it to the leadership of a nation.

But there is more reason for becoming a Republican than simply joining a rescue operation, no matter how challenging that task may be. I believe that the Republican party is in an excellent position to make a new breakthrough to political leadership in this country—by concentrating on the rebuilding of our state and local governments, by bringing new imagination to the problems of urban America.

Such a Republican party can become the party of adventure and excitement. It can break new ground in American politics. It can become a great innovating force—an instrument more flexible than the complacent Democratic majority in exploring and developing the political challenges of the future to serve better our people and ourselves.

Seen in this light, the Republican 1965 victories in New York and Philadelphia take on a new significance. At a moment when the Republican party was in grave danger of losing its relevance to an ever more urban America, moderate and liberal Republicans have provided a stunning breakthrough in the citadel of decaying Democratic strength. At a time when the American electorate is undergoing a "silent revolution" at its base, when a new generation, demanding a new purpose and style in its politics, is rapidly coming to power, moderate and liberal Republicans have provided a leadership that cuts across the partisan divisions of distant decades—a leadership with a generational appeal that may well capture the future of American politics.

The election of 1965 has important implications for the Democratic party as well. In traditional centers of Democratic strength, the majority party was put in the position of defending the tired programs of the past. The national Democratic leadership was identified with the discredited and uninspired record of urban machine politics. President Johnson rationalized his endorsement with the comment that he always prefers a Democrat to a Republican. Vice-President Humphrey moved perfunctorily from campaign to campaign, the dispenser of official Democratic blessings. Senator Robert Kennedy was personally involved in the unsuccessful Beame campaign. It is clear that party loyalty, national prestige, and familiar personalities are forces which can be overcome by the promise of bold and creative government. In 1965 it was the Republicans who embodied this promise in New York and Philadelphia. And as a result, as columnist and scholar Max Lerner has written, the 1965 election "marks the possible breakup of the coalition—Catholics, Jews, Negroes, trade unions—which has given the Democrats the edge in almost every big city since the New Deal." Republicans must continue to capitalize on this opportunity and this challenge.

A new breed of Republicans have won in the cities. They have shattered the conventional wisdom of an obsolescent partisanship. They have shown Republicans the expanding opportunity and possibility in the population heartland of America. They are beginning to give form and substance to a Republican program for the urban areas. Inevitable as these events and directions may seem to some they have just begun to be perceived by Republicans nationally.

Now is the time for other dynamic young leaders to join Republican ranks—representatives of what the Republican party of tomorrow must be. We hope that you will share in our efforts to give a new Republican party both the courage to win and the courage to lead.

Sincerely,

John S. Saloma III
President: The Ripon Society

Other Ripon Society Publications include:

"A Call to Excellence in Leadership—An Open Letter to the New Generation of Republicans"	January, 1964
"The Republican Party and Civil Rights: A Continuing Commitment," prepared by the Ripon Society for the Critical Issues Council of the Republican Citizens Committee	April, 1964
"A Declaration of Conscience—A Call for Return to Basic Republican Principles"	July, 1964
"A New Republican Mandate—Preliminary Analysis of the 1964 Elections"	November, 1964
"The Republican Governors' Association: The Case for a Third Force," Ripon Society Report and Recommendations to the Republican Governors	December, 1964
"Election '64—Report on the Style, Strategy and Issues of the 1964 Campaign and State by State Analysis of the Results, with Recommendations"	January, 1965
"Government for Tomorrow—a Proposal for the Unconditional Sharing of Federal Tax Revenues with State and Local Government," jointly prepared by the Republican Governors' Association and the Ripon Society	July, 1965
"A Second Mandate to Republicans—An Analysis of the 1965 Elections"	November, 1965
"China '66: Containment and Contact—A Ripon policy statement"	April, 1966
The Ripon *Forum,* Newsletter of the Ripon Society	Monthly, beginning in 1965

Information on receiving any of the above publications or on subscribing to the Ripon *Forum* and future publications of the Ripon Society may be obtained by writing to:

The Ripon Society, P.O. Box 138
Cambridge, Massachusetts 02138
Tel. 617-491-4180